BLACK
ANTHOLOGY

ADULT ADOPTEES CLAIM THEIR SPACE

A Diverse Exploration
of the Black Adoptee Journey

Edited and Compiled By:
Susan Harris O'Connor MSW,
Diane René Christian, Mei-Mei Akwai Ellerman PhD

Black Anthology: Adult Adoptees Claim Their Space
Edited and Compiled By: Susan Harris O'Connor MSW, Diane
René Christian, Mei-Mei Akwai Ellerman PhD

First Print Edition: 2016

ISBN-13: 978-1539395188
ISBN-10: 1539395189

Cover Design & Formatting by:Streetlight Graphics

The AN-YA Project

An-Ya and Her Diary: The Novel (April, 2012)
An-Ya and Her Diary: Reader & Parent Guide (April, 2013)
Perpetual Child: Adult Adoptee Anthology (November, 2013)
Dear Wonderful You, Letters to Adopted & Fostered Youth (2014)
Flip the Script: Adult Adoptee Anthology (2015)
Black Anthology: Adult Adoptees Claim Their Space (2016)

For more information on the AN-YA Project visit:
www.anyaproject.com

TABLE OF CONTENTS

You may trod me in the very dirt
But still, like dust, I'll rise.

-Maya Angelou
And Still I Rise, Random House (New York, NY), 1978

FOREWORD

Black.
Black, adopted and fostered.
We are beautiful.
Black and beautiful.

THIS ANTHOLOGY CELEBRATES THE VOICE of a missing racial population which disproportionately accounts for much of the global adoption mosaic. We represent adult adopted individuals who live throughout the world.

We are diverse. In no way could anyone simply summarize our beginnings. The historical, socio-political contexts from which countries we come from are culturally varied. Our identities are connected to Haiti, Germany, Ethiopia, Vietnam, Korea, Sweden, Canada, the USA and many other places not mentioned within this publication.

People who identify as Black adoptees are vaguely known within both adoption circles as well as universal discussions. We are just beginning to be introduced to one another. This anthology allows for the opportunity to see the rich diversity of a people; the uniqueness within the individual stories. Inside this book, you will read the depth of struggle, and the pure grace, dignity and accomplishments achieved, sometimes connected to the privileges afforded us while in the midst of insurmountable odds.

Years ago, I became extremely cognizant that there was a need for this collection of voices. Over the past twenty years, I have performed my autobiographical narratives around the country to initiate productive conversations on difficult subjects such as—complex identities, racism, foster care and transracial adoption.

Rarely though—do I see or experience what I would refer to as 'racial/ ethnic adult adoptee mirroring' in that I see and/or have an opportunity to meet and form community with other Black adult adoptees.

I am by birth a Jewish, and tri-racial (Black, white, Seminole Indian) person who, after a year in foster care, was adopted in 1964 by white Jewish parents and raised in a predominately white community in Massachusetts. The only other Black transracially adopted persons I knew until my late 20s were my two non-biological adopted brothers. It was an environment, later learned through reflection, which left my identity in a vulnerable state.

When I began my professional career as an educator, I sought to find and form meaningful relationships with adult Black transracially adopted persons. I hoped, as a professional, I would meet others like me.

Yet, as time continues, and as I approach my mid 50's, I better understand this ongoing challenge of meeting adult Black transracially adopted persons. It is a symptom of a much wider issue which speaks to the ongoing lack of adult Black representation in general. Why is this?

Why is it that Black adoptees of all backgrounds aren't seen in numbers when I move around in spaces?

Why is it that relatively few are known in adoption literature?

If it wasn't for social media, I could easily believe that there are very few Black adult adoptees that exist. At times this void has left me speechless. There are Black adoptees, spanning multiple generations, who still lack 'racial/ethnic adoptee mirroring'. This 'mirroring' experience has been a crucial and critical component to my healing journey. It has allowed me to speak safely to others. Others who identify through *lived* experiences of not only the positives but that of the struggle and oppression at the intersection of Black/race, multi-racial, adoption, transracial adoption, religion, nationality, gender and age.

Isn't this an experience we should have?

I hope this anthology provides Black adoptees with the opportunity to have a collective presence in the fostered and adoption community. My goal is to create a forum in which we can share our experiences, passion, expertise and scholarly works both via the written and spoken word.

Never in my wildest dreams did I think this literary force would come to fruition. It is my distinct honor and pleasure to assist in gathering such a brilliant group of people whom I deeply admire. I have longed for this moment.

Let us salute the courage which unites the remarkable achievements of a collective race of adopted persons.

Let us begin to learn from those who have long lived the experience and whose contributions are uncensored by neither parent nor institution. Through those who are able to share with the world a much needed glimpse of our humanity which spans beyond the social construct of race.

Let us continue to be open to diversity. Let us begin to honor diversity within the Black African Diaspora.

-Susan Harris O'Connor, MSW

ROSEMARIE PEÑA

BLACK GERMANS: REUNIFICATION AND BELONGING IN DIASPORA

"Be confident in your blackness. One of the great changes that's occurred in our country since I was your age is the realization there's no one way to be black. Take it from somebody who's seen both sides of debate about whether I'm black enough. ... There's no straitjacket, there's no constraints, there's no litmus test for authenticity."

- President Barack Obama, 2016
Howard University Commencement.

THE VOICES OF THE DUAL-HERITAGE, biracial, middle-aged adoptees from Germany who were born during the aftermath of WWII are beginning to emerge in public discourse and are a relatively new topic of interest in adoption scholarship. My personal journey as a member of this finite, historical cohort and my long-term engagement with the international community of Black Germans, has not only impassioned my research, it also deepened my concern for the well-being of contemporary, culturally displaced, Black children. As an adoptee, scholar, and as the president of the Black German Heritage and Research Association (BGHRA), I have been privileged to represent the interests and concerns of Black German adoptees internationally. Scholars who write about international adoption often mention the humanitarian efforts to rescue orphaned children from a war-torn Europe while attributing its institutionalization to the *Act of September 26, 1961*, an amendment to the *Immigration & Naturalization Act* (INA) initiated by Harry and Bertha Holt that facilitated the adoptions of Korean children. The thousands of Black Germans who were systematically expelled from their country of origin and dispersed to

13

other European countries and the U.S.—simply because of the color of their skin, are rarely, if ever, mentioned in adoption literature.

Between 1945 and 1956, an estimated 150,000 children were born to soldiers of the occupying forces and German women. More than 9,000 were the children of African American and Moroccan soldiers (Lemke-Muniz de Faria 2003). There are no definitive statistics, but by 1968 experts estimate that in the two decades following the War as many as seven thousand biracial German children were adopted by middle-class African Americans, many of whom were military couples who were living in Germany at the time. The numbers are approximate since German census records do not account for race. All of the adoptions were closed. Notably, Black Germans are the only known historical cohort of foreign-born children to have been adopted to the United States almost exclusively by African Americans.

Mabel Grammer, a correspondent for a Baltimore based newspaper, *The Afro-American,* and her husband, a U.S. Naval officer stationed in Germany, adopted twelve of the Afro German children and Mabel launched a press campaign encouraging other African American couples to adopt. It is estimated that she facilitated over five hundred adoptions. Mabel Grammer's initiative became known as the "Brown Baby Plan," and the children she placed were labeled the "Grammer Babies." Many of the children, whose plight was publicized extensively in Germany and in African American newspapers and magazines were adopted "by proxy" to sympathetic African American married couples who were able to provide evidence of their education and economic stability. At the same time, unknown numbers of Black German children were institutionalized, adopted, or fostered within a divided Germany or sent to families willing to care for them in neighboring Scandinavian countries (Lemke, 2003).

Black German adoptees residing in the U.S. today are roughly between 60 and 70 years old and identify as CIS male and female as well as LGBTQ. Many are now parents and grandparents, and reside in all regions of the United States—in rural, urban, and suburban communities. Most grew up in middle-to-upper middle class civilian or military households. Some who were placed in civilian families attended segregated public and private schools. Those who grew up on military campuses were in many ways sheltered from the overt experiences of racism that plagued civilian society in the 1960s and were socialized and educated in racially and culturally diverse environments. Adoptees who grew up in military families often describe the transition to civilian society as having been a particularly daunting one. While there is no monolithic Black German adoptee experience, many themes that emerge in their conversations are indeed consistent with those that appear in the adoption literature focusing on other adoptive groups. They discuss matters of identity, culture, and birth-family reunification.

Black Germans have wrestled with the same grief and losses as other adoptees associated with the involuntary separation from their first mothers. Many regret the loss of the German language and culture. For some, documenting their U.S. citizenship is still precarious and a few are known to have been deported. Others mention the desire for the bi-national recognition that they believe would be achieved through dual citizenship. Missing and sealed birth and adoption records make identity determination and locating original family members extremely difficult and for some these obstacles appear to be insurmountable. Language and cultural differences, along with racism sometimes complicate adoptees' ability to establish meaningful social relationships with their birth-family members post-reunion. While some adoptees describe a satisfying reunification experience, others share that they have faced rejection or the discovery that after delaying their searches until their adoptive parents passed away, their biological mothers and /or fathers have also already died.

Similar to many transracial adoptees, Black Germans often assert that they grew up feeling isolated within their extended adoptive families. As foreign, biracial children whose very existence was evidence of a crime when they first arrived in the United States, many argue they experience race and racism differently than their African American family members and peers. Black Germans, like other biracial children born to African American soldiers and native women after war, must come to terms with the reality that they may never see themselves visually reflected anywhere within their Adoption Kinship Networks (Baden, 2015). Black Germans endured and are challenged to overcome many of the same microaggressions that Amanda Baden discusses in her most recent article,

'Do You Know Your Real Parents?' and *Other Adoption Microaggressions*, in addition to those that accompany attitudes consistent with anti-black racism, anti-miscegenation, classism, and colorism. Growing up during in the midst of the Civil Rights and Cold War Eras, many describe contextually specific insults associated with their German heritage and the stigma of illegitimacy.

There has not yet been an ethnographic exploration of Black German-American adoption experiences and the few existing memoirs and historiographic documentary films primarily depict abusive childhoods and failed reunions. These few stories are not emblematic of a collective experience. As Chimamanda Ngozi Adichie notes, "Stories matter. Many stories matter. Stories have been used to dispossess and to malign, but stories can also be used to empower and to humanize. Stories can break the dignity of a people, but stories can also repair that broken dignity" (2009). The vast majority of adoptees I have come to know over the more than fifteen years that I have served as an international community leader and participant observer/moderator in Black German social media networks, have come to terms with their adopted, racial, and ethnic identities, enjoy positive family relationships, and lead productive and fulfilling lives.

It is the salience of an adopted identity and the desire to learn more about what it means to be a dual-heritage, Black person of German descent that precipitates the sharing of adoptee life stories in Black German online networks and forums. Adoptees who join these networks discover that Black people have a very long history in Germany extending back many generations. Black German is an inclusive term that includes persons living in or connected to Germany with ethnic roots stemming not only from the United States, but also from a number of African countries. Among others, these include Ghana, Mali, Nigeria, Cameroon, Senegal, Namibia, Ethiopia, and Eritrea. The post WWII adoptees are also not the only appreciable group of biracial children who were born in Germany to German women and foreign Black troops. Tina Campt writes extensively about the "Rhineland Children," in her seminal text, *Other Germans - Black Germans and the Politics of Race, Gender, and Memory in the Third Reich* (2004). The youth were sterilized as soon as they reached puberty in accordance with Germany's racial purity laws. Many simply disappeared.

Liberian-German Hans Jürgen Massaquoi's memoir, *Destined to Witness* (2001), describes his childhood experience growing up in Nazi Germany and surviving the War. After migrating to the U.S., he became the Managing Editor of Ebony Magazine and the Associate Editor of Jet Magazine. Adoptees who imagine what their lives might have been like had they remained in Germany discover through the memoirs of contemporary peers like Ika Hügel Marshall (Invisible Woman, 2008) and from the groundbreaking anthology, *Showing Our Colors: Afro-German Women Speak Out* (Opitz et al., 1991) that as Molefe Asante argues, Black people in Germany, regardless of ethnic origin and place of birth are "culturally dislocated."

In her keynote, *Geteilte Geschichte* (Shared/Divided History), given at the inaugural convention of the BGHRA, often described as a watershed event, Noah Sow reminded the audience that the mass deportation of Black German children through the instrument of adoption has had transnational implications. Addressing the adoptees, she said:

Step by step, we are coming to understand that there is a reason, a link to why our older generations in Germany grew up isolated, alienated from other Black people—with the same pain and the key question that could not and cannot be safely enunciated, "You all do not identify with me. Where can I find someone who does? And with whom can I identify?"

We are coming to understand why this has been so. Why most of the Black German kids in the 1970s and 1980s didn't have anybody to turn to.

Because they had taken you away. You would have been our sisters, our mothers, our aunts. Our teachers, our deans, our doctors, our librarians, our social workers, our judges, our pilots, our nurses, our neighbors. We've been missing you a great deal.

Sow's talk was sponsored by Debra Abell, in memoriam of her parents, Irmgard and James W. Tanner. Mr. Tanner, an African American soldier, met and married his German wife, with whom he returned to the United States and created a family, during the same period that Scandinavian Airlines was delivering groups of Black German children to their waiting African American families across the Atlantic Ocean.

The idea that Black German adoptees, particularly those who were adopted into military families, often grew up in communities with their non-adopted biracial peers who conceivably outnumber them, is another topic of interest that has not yet been fully explored. The BGHRA conventions have been remarkable in that they have brought together representatives of the Black German Diaspora with the scholars who write about them. The filmed keynote and panel presentations spanning three consecutive years are available on the BGHRA website. These include not only scholarly papers, but also life narratives that reveal the diversity of Black German experiences. Importantly, they document the ongoing efforts of adoptees to reunify in life and discourse with their globally distributed ethnic peers. For many adoptees, establishing social relationships with other Black Germans is highly valued. For some, these encounters whether on or off-line are the only type of reunification possible. There is much hidden within the historical Black German adoption experience(s) that more closely examined will undoubtedly contribute to a more nuanced understanding of the race, culture, and nation in adoption.

Works Cited

Adichie, Chimamanda Ngozi. *The Danger of a Single Story*. Vol. 2009. N.p., 2009. Film. TEDGlobal.

Asante, Molefe Kete. "Afro-Germans and the Problems of Cultural Location | Dr. Molefi Kete Asante." N.p., n.d. Web. 10 June 2014.

Baden, A.l. "'Do You Know Your Real Parents?' and Other Adoption Microaggressions." *Adoption Quarterly* 19.1 (2016): 1–25. *EBSCOhost*. Web.

Campt, Tina. *Other Germans Black Germans and the Politics of Race, Gender, and Memory in the Third Reich*. Ann Arbor: University of Michigan, 2004. Print.

Fehrenbach, Heide. *Race after Hitler: Black Occupation Children in Postwar Germany and America*. Princeton, N.J.; Woodstock: Princeton UP, 2007. Print.

Griffin, Regina. *Brown Babies: The Mischlingskinder Story*. N.p., 2011. Film.

Hügel-Marshall, Ika. *Invisible Woman: Growing Up Black in Germany*. Peter Lang, 2008. Print.

Kirst, Michaela. *Brown Babies: Deutschlands Verlorene Kinder (Germany's Forgotten Children)*. N.p., 2011. Film.

Lemke Muniz de Faria, Yara-Colette Lemke. "'Germany's "Brown Babies" Must Be Helped! Will You?': U.S. Adoption Plans for Afro-German Children, 1950-1955." *Callaloo* 26.2 (2003): 342–362. Print.

Obama, Barack. "Remarks by the President at Howard University Commencement Ceremony." *whitehouse.gov*. N.p., 7 May 2016. Web. 30 July 2016.

Opitz, May, Katharina Oguntoye, and Dagmar Schultz. *Showing Our Colors: Afro-German Women Speak Out*. Amherst: University of Massachusetts Press, 1991. Print.

Sow, Noah. "Geteilte Geschichte." Convention of the Black German Historical and Research Association. German Historical Institute-DC. 2011.

HANNA WALLENSTEEN

WHERE DO YOU COME FROM?

I WAS BORN IN ETHIOPIA AND adopted to Sweden as an infant. I have no contact with my birth family. All ties were cut at the time of my adoption in the early seventies. I don't know who they are, where they live or even if they are alive. I don't know their language or culture and most likely I will never know any of it. All I know is that for some reason they could not take care of me. And that most likely, I look like them.

I do not look like my Swedish adoptive family. Not at all. But I was taught to be color blind. I was told that the color of my skin was of no importance. That my adoptive family would always love me regardless of how I looked. That we were a regular Swedish family like everyone else. That I would always be Swedish and that Sweden is probably the most anti-racist country in the world.

That I need not think about where I come from.

The seventies

Strangers would look at me and my adoptive family at the playground, on the bus, at the doctor's or anywhere else. They would ask where I came from and my adoptive parents would explain that I was adopted from Ethiopia to Sweden. The strangers responded with a mixture of pity and admiration. Pity for me to come from such a God forsaken place of war and famine. Admiration for my parents to take on such a poor creature as I to live in healthy, wealthy Sweden.

The strangers would touch my hair, commenting on how odd it felt and ask if it was possible to wash. They would touch my cheeks and say they wished that they had such a suntan themselves. They would ask endless questions about my short stature. How could it be that I was so short? Did my adoptive parents not feed me well? Long answers on proteins and vitamins. How strange that a healthy eating child did not grow taller! But with my good adoptive parents' love I would surely grow to become just as tall and bright as they were. The strangers patted my head and repeated how blessed I was.

At the age of eight I tried to count them all.

Dear God,

Thank you for my mother (1) and my father (2) and my sister (3). I don't think they believe in you, God, but they are really good people anyway. Thank you for letting me have food on the table every day (4). Thank you for water (5), heat (6), electricity (7) and the roof over my head (8). And for the walls (9). And my bed (10) and all the furniture in our house (11). Thank you for my school (12), my teacher (13) and for all my class mates (13+17=30). Thank you for my closest relatives and neighbors (30+11+7=48). Thank you for my clothes and for my toys (48 + not sure how many, I'll count them tomorrow). My plan was to continue with thanks for my choir and my gymnastics, for summer vacations and Christmas gifts, for nature, freedom, justice, peace, health and wealth, but usually I fell asleep too fast. The few times I reached the end of my list I had a lingering feeling that there were essential blessings that I had forgotten to count.

No. I could not count them all.

The eighties

Strangers would look at me at school, on the bus, at the doctor's or anywhere else. They would ask me where I came from and I would explain that I was adopted from Ethiopia to Sweden. The strangers responded with a mixture of pity and reassurance. Pity for me to come from such a God forsaken place of war and famine. And reassurance that I was fortunate to have ended up here in healthy, wealthy Sweden. I remembered to say thank you and counted some of my blessings to the strangers.

The strangers touched my hair, and commented on how odd it felt. They touched my cheeks and expressed how they wished that they had such a suntan themselves. They asked about my short stature suggesting I should get medical help in order to grow a little taller.

At the age of fourteen and fifteen I got daily injections of growth hormone, provided by public health care, in order to help me grow to the top of my potential. I gained an extra inch, finishing at a total height of 59 inches, which was quite a disappointment to me as well as to the doctors.

My adoptive family always loved me, regardless of what I looked like.

The nineties

Africans who had migrated to Sweden as refugees would look at me at work, on the bus, at the doctor's or anywhere else. They would ask me where I came from and I would explain that I was adopted from Ethiopia to Sweden. The immigrants from Africa responded with a mixture of envy and disappointment. Envy for me to have grown up in such a blessed place of health and wealth. And disappointment that I did not know any of my Ethiopian language, culture or heritage.

The immigrant African strangers never touched my cheeks and they didn't seem to notice my short stature. But they were quick to inform me that I needed to do something about my hair. Until then there had been no hairdressers for afro hair in Sweden. Now I could finally "relax" my hair into thin, straight hair. I let my hair loose, let it slip down over my eyes and casually threw it back, totally forgetting what I really looked like. I was truly color blind. The color of my skin was of no importance and my family loved me regardless of how I looked. I would always be Swedish and in my mind I was just as tall and bright as my adoptive family. Why would I think about where I came from?

Until some skin headed neo-Nazi passed me by at work, on the bus, at the doctor's or anywhere else, reminding me loud and clear that I was a f***ing n***er who should go back to where I came from and climb back into the trees.

A new millennium

White men would look at me at the night club, on the bus, at the doctor's or anywhere else. They would ask me where I came from and I would explain that I was adopted from Ethiopia to Sweden. The white men responded with a mixture of excitement and rejection. Excitement with the assumption that I came from an exotic place of primitive drums and dancing. And rejection with the first rays of sunlight, as my straightened hair went back to its original frizziness and the thought of presenting me to their mothers seemed too inappropriate. The white men thought that the color of my skin was of no importance to them. But they said that their mothers wanted them to have a regular Swedish family like everyone else.

The white men did not touch my hair. We pretended it wasn't there. The white men did not kiss my cheek. They pretended we had never met. The white men said nothing about my short stature. But they enjoyed the excitement of a body that was so "petite".

Strangers in Ethiopia would look at me at the guest house, on the bus, at the swimming pool or anywhere else. They would ask me where I came from and my translator would explain that I had been adopted to Sweden from Ethiopia. The strangers in Ethiopia kissed my cheeks and let my hair be. Sometimes they were the same height as I.

At the story of my adoption the strangers in Ethiopia responded with a mixture of pity and reassurance. Pity that for some reason my birth family could not take care of me. And reassurance that I would always be Ethiopian anyway.

2016

Strangers look at me, my husband and our children at the playground, on the bus, at the doctor's or anywhere else. My husband is white and our children have light brown skin and curls from a fairy tale. They look like a combination of us.

When I am with my husband, nobody will ask where I come from. Swedes have been taught to be color blind. That the color of my skin is of no importance. That my white husband could probably love me regardless of how I look. That we are a regular Swedish family like everyone else. Therefore they need not think about where I come from.

But when I am not with my husband, strangers will ask me where I come from. The strangers will look as if they think they are doing me a favor. As if asking a dark skinned stranger about where she comes from is an anti-racist action. I was born in Ethiopia and adopted to Sweden as an infant. I have no contact with my birth family. All ties were cut at the time of my adoption in the early seventies. I don't know who they are, where they live or even if they are alive. I don't know their language or culture and most likely I will never know any of it. All I know is that for some reason they could not take care of me.

The strangers respond with a mixture of pity and reassurance. Pity for me to come from such a God forsaken place of war and famine. And reassurance that I am fortunate to have ended up here in healthy, wealthy Sweden.

The strangers touch my children's hair, comment on how beautiful it is and wonder if it's difficult to wash. They touch my children's cheeks and say they wish that they had such a suntan themselves. They have endless questions on their short stature. How could it possibly be that healthy eating children could be so short? Perhaps they need medical help?

I find myself struggling between saying thanks and shouting shut up. I hear myself count my blessings, while strangers count the curls in my children's hair. I watch my children being reduced to exotic little creatures, as I tread water in an ocean of privilege. I wish these strangers would tell me about where they come from themselves, count their own blessings, or at least ask me where I am going. Perhaps we are going the same way? But too often I meet healthy, wealthy Swedes patting my children's heads, repeating how beautiful their hair is. Forcing my children to say their thanks and start counting their blessings.

I swim in an ocean of white privilege. I have a family that always loves me. I speak fluent Swedish without any accent. I have a name I never need to spell out to anyone. My parents are rich and my family is good looking. I count my blessings as I swim in the Ocean of White Privilege.

I have dark skinned sisters and brothers who swim for their lives in the Mediterranean Sea. They are swimming the dreams of their short statured grandparents. I have aunts and uncles with thick afro hair, drowning with their dreams of health and wealth. Skinny young nephews counting the names they know of European football players as they suffocate in cargo spaces. Brown eyed nieces in asylum housings, waiting in vain, while Adele sings *Hello* from the other side.

The former skinheads have combed their hair and covered their swastika tattoos with white collar shirts. Their blonde sisters treasure the dreams of their skull-measuring great grandparents. Their bright brothers have changed random racist name calling into structured nationalist party programs. Their tall aunts and uncles have sugar coated their messages into Christian traditions and cultural values, gaining an alarming amount of seats in the Swedish parliament. And while their skinny young nephews' burn down asylum housings, their blue-eyed nieces continue counting inches and curls—in probably the most anti-racist country in the world.

Of course I need to think about where I come from.

MILTON WASHINGTON

THE KOREANS OF MISHKIN'S PHARMACY

THE WIND RUSHED HARD FROM the Hudson, slicing through the dozen of us huddled at our Harlem bus stop. An elderly Black man stood just below the iconic Mishkin's Pharmacy sign. Tall and distinguished like the dying breed of Harlem's graying statesmen, he stood with his mustache and chin high. I thought he might have owned the place.

"Excuse me sir. Is Mishkin's yours?" I asked pointing up to the rusted-blue neon sign that stood almost as tall as the five-story building.

"*Humph,*" his body jerked with a hiccup of contempt. "I wish it was, but them damn Ko-Reans done got to it already."

Ahhhh... "*Ko-Reans.*" *Just like Black folk say* "*Po-lice.*"

And then he was off and running, speaking with the kind of candor that only comes within like company—an older Black man passing on what's what in the world to a younger one. I validated his outrage with a bit of humor.

"I should have known," I said with a slow shake of my head like my grandmother used to do when expressing resignation. "First they get the dry cleaners, then the delis and soul food joints, and now our pharmacies too? It's gettin' out of hand!" I laughed. "It's like they're the new Jews or something!"

"Jews stick to real estate, they ain't tryin' to be all up in your face. But them Ko-Reans? They takin' that dolla' from our black hands to they yellow hands, and nasty as all hell doing so, especially they women!" he snapped.

"Oh yeah?" I asked with questioning eyes, encouraging him for an explanation.

"*Yessa*, that Ko-Rean man's wife is the damn devil. Treat Black folks like we ain't shit!" he said with a curled lip.

"Sounds like you've had a couple run-ins with her," I said, wanting more.

"Ain't just me she got a problem with, it's anybody Black."

We went back and forth in agreement on how those "Ko-Reans" could be among the most racist of all the Asians. He spoke with good observation and authority because his experiences went well beyond the businesses of Harlem; they went all the way back to his days as a Marine in the Korean War. He explained how the men were mostly quiet in their objection to the American presence, caring only for that therapeutic US dollar. But the women? Protective of their culture like a pack of lionesses in a pride.

"You can't hide hate in the eyes," he said tapping a gloved finger on his temple. And as we clutched hooks on the Bronx-bound bus he continued about the women of Korea. "Man, those women hated us. Cursed us, spat at our feet and called us all kinds of names we couldn't understand. And after all these years, all I remember of their language are their words for "hello", "thank you", and that word I heard just about every day from those nasty women—they word for *nigga – gum-dingi*"!

As he spoke I thought of the famous image of Little Rock desegregating their schools. The one from 1957 with Elizabeth Eckford, a Black girl in the foreground walking in a skirt, studiously holding a notebook in her arm with grief in her face and courage in her stride. The backdrop, lined with the Army National Guard, wielding rifles and batons as white students milled about in an angry air reminiscent of a lynching. Directly behind Elizabeth, three white teenagers followed with scowls of disdain targeted at the young girl, the shortest girl captured with her mouth wide open, probably yelling words of hate common for the time and place.

"Nigger!

Gumdingi...

Maybe the old Harlem man was right because you *can* see hate in their eyes. He's awfully perceptive because that's exactly how the men and women of South Korea were—the men indifferent and resigned, the women acrimonious and vile to the intrusive Americans, especially those *Black* Americans.

I know exactly what he's talking about because I remember that hatred in a way that no historian or geopolitical expert could ever know. I know not because I make weekly trips to Manhattan's Korea Town or have Korean friends. It's not because I make my house guests take off their shoes or put *kimchi* on my pizza and eggs. I know because Korea is where I was born.

First language.

First culture.

First mother.

She, a resilient and loving mother who so happened to be a prostitute forced by her country and the US military to choose the color of soldier she'd serve. Her choice to be exclusively with Black soldiers made her a three-fold outcast—prostitute, lover of Black men, and a mother of a Black child. So I guess that makes me a bit like Elizabeth Eckford—surrounded by the angst, contempt, and hate of a majority. But my majority was not a community or a region of a country, but rather an *entire* country, one that never claimed me with a birth certificate or citizenship.

So when I told the man on the bus who I really was, a Black boy born to a *kiji-chon* or a camptown prostitute in South Korea, who roamed his town with a pack of homeless kids fighting, stealing, and drinking while his mother worked long hours, he was taken aback. When I explained that one day, during a temporary stay at an orphanage, I stowed away into the lives of a Black Army family from Texas, he became physically shaken. And when I told him of the memoir I was writing, a compelling story of isolation and identity, but most of all a story of love, the love of two mothers that insulated that boy caught between worlds for the rest of his wonderful life, he had questions.

"Adopted from *Ko-Rea*, huh?" the man asked somberly, nearly in a whisper.

"Yep. I was eight."

"How about your birth mother, have you seen her since?" he asked with eyes bouncing around my face examining every feature, almost as if he was searching for more than just an answer.

"No. The last time I saw her was a day after she dropped me off at St. Vincent's Orphanage for Amer-Asians. She hugged me long and tight and whispered in my ear and told me to be strong."

"That's a powerful story, young man, that needs to be told. A lot of my partners from the service left little kids over there just like you and ain't nobody said a word about them!" he said as he balled his hand to a fist. "God bless you, young man, and get that story out!" he commanded, shaking a finger at me.

A lot of my partners from the service left little kids over there just like you...

Those words...

I've always wondered about the stories of soldiers who left children behind—seeds planted in such charred ground. Who were these men? How were they able to live out their lives knowing they'd left children to grow in such inhospitable lands? As questions thumped in my head like the Reggaeton beats of the Dominicans' minivans rolling by, I found myself revisiting the elder man's features: The glimmers of his still-athletic body under his trench—athletic like mine. His rich, dark, earthly skin that could have hailed from the Carolinas was perfect stock to mix with the hue of a Korean woman, to produce my special blend of brown with reddish undertones. And how about the anger that seemed to singe every word? Was it simply the kind of anger that many of us Black men mature into like white hairs of a beard? Or was it something more, deeper and more profound? Maybe it's the rage of a long-held secret hidden from spouse, children and friends. The kind of secret that makes a man give up his liquor, go cold turkey, because of a drunken leak of that secret on a hazy night with fellow vets. And what if it's the variety of secret that comes packed full of visuals that can't be shaken with work or a hobby, images that constantly scroll in your head as you lie for sleep and cause guilty pangs to your conscience and an ever-present malaise in the eyes that no smile can hide? Because behind that false cheer is knowledge of a wide-faced, eager-eyed, hopeful little boy left behind reaching, screaming, *and yearning* for his unknown father, his *Appa*.

As the bus hissed into my stop, I found myself almost regretting opening the exchange with the old man and eager to disengage. Sometimes you have to be careful of what you ask for, especially here in New York.

His name...I thought. *What if?* I wondered as my grip tightened on the hanging strap.

I found myself hesitant by the idea to ask for his name. Did I really want to know? I've been known to have strange but fortunate luck.

What if? What if we shared a name?

"Yes sir I will, I'll get that book out ASAP," I shot back and we shook hands and I exited the bus.

Walking towards the Starbucks a shiver ran down my spine, nudging my regret of not asking for the man's name aside, replaced by another fear that shook me even deeper to my core.

Am I really trying to dig and excavate my past for full display to the world? I wondered.

And what about my mother? I recently discovered that she's alive at the ripe age of eighty-nine, and in 1998, she migrated to the States with her three Korean daughters, who were born in '55, '56 and '65—my older half-sisters. What if she'd like to leave those stories of her life in Korea buried and out of sight from her *current* world? How would my Korean sisters react if my story makes it big, maybe even making it to the Big Screen, as I recount such mature topics implicating our mother through the blissfully innocent eyes of a child? And how about her health? At eighty-nine, could she handle *my* truth? And what about me? What if I discover that by writing this book there's so much more to my story, parts redacted by my heart out of necessity, buried deep in my psyche like drums of uranium in the hills? But what if splinters of memories arranged in anesthetized logic were to realign into a more caustic sequence, landing me in a padded room or even worse, in a swan dive off a bridge?

You see, my foundation and strength are derived from a simple idea: I've survived a dramatic and even traumatic life with my emotions intact because I was a child who knew I was loved. First by my biological mother, my *Umma*, and then by the woman who became my adoptive mother, my angel, Gwendolyn Washington. But what if? What if my memories are self-preserving, drastically altered and deeply departed from reality? What if my mother didn't actually love me the way I thought she had?

What if?

NATASHA ORLANDO

FILLING THE SILENCE

YOU SIT AND THINK FOR a long time before you begin to type about your life. You are adopted. Your adoptive family is white. You are black, or Black, or African American, or an Africana person. To put it in scholarly terms, you're a member of the African Diaspora. For the sake of brevity, though, and with a nod to your lifelong status as a citizen born in the United States, let's just say you're black. No. *Black*.

The reason for the capital letter is because Blackness is a consciously political identity, not the mere designation of dark skin. In order to insist that this identity be respected as encompassing not just physical traits, but also culture, politics, language, social and economic status, and all those intersecting phenomena that make us fully and three-dimensionally human, you must first have immersed yourself in the world(s) of Blackness. You may have read fiercely, perhaps partnered by choice within the Diaspora, lived or worked in neighborhoods heavily populated by Black folks, and dived headfirst into Black food, dialects, spirituality, and music. But most of all you've done the thing you couldn't help but do: You've walked around every day of your life in the dark skin and physical markings of Blackness.

That means that when people see you, they immediately know your background. They know you are Black. The nuclear bomb you've juggled since you were barely able to speak up for yourself is the reality that once others recognize your background, they treat you accordingly. You are never sure if they register you as a superstar athlete, an amazing culture-shaping musician, or the embodiment of every negative stereotype trotted out about Black people on the 24-hour news cycle. You never know if the reception will be kindly or dangerous. You ask yourself each time you walk into a room, if you are safe, if your dignity will remain intact after each exchange, or if all the smiles toward which you were walking a moment ago will suddenly disappear. You tremble any time you pass by the Police. There is no one in your immediate family who has or ever will experience this, and so, they cannot help you. You must navigate each encounter with the monsters of race and discrimination alone, from the moment you are old enough to walk out of your house.

Don't forget, you are a transracial adoptee (TRA). Let's say you are a first generation TRA, adopted back in the earliest, experimental days of the practice. Every time you go back home, you are drafted into a full time job as Integrator. In fact, going home means that you are often the only Black adult in the room. Entering the neighborhood of your childhood generates stares and invasive questions. "Home" means Never Having to See Black People.

Perhaps coming home even generates denigrating remarks from white members of your family about your body shape, Black cultural touchstones you hold dear, or how you wear your hair. These remarks will be made to sound like jokes, or good-natured teasing. After all, these are the people who love you more than anyone else in the world does, and who raised you with all the attending sacrifices. They can joke around with you about your body, your perceived worth, and your very sense of self. They can denigrate the politics that brought your liberation, turn their noses up at the Soul Music that saved your life, and insist that the only God there is looks like them. They're family.

But wait. Should you write about that?

Is it appropriate to put down on paper that slowly over time, the words of encouragement that you needed, the sense of worth and belonging bestowed by family, slowly became more and more scarce? If you are one of those TRAs whose parents loved you only if you acted appropriately, and allowed them to take the easy way out instead of standing with you as you faced down systemic and institutional racism, is it all right to publish that fact for the world to read? You've felt, to be honest, that you lost your family years ago, when you, a mere teenager, were no longer able to carry the adult responsibility of staying alive, let alone thriving, in a culture bent on Black destruction, all while maintaining a perfect façade. Is it all right to share that? Or, does revealing those raw, difficult stories make you ungrateful, disloyal, and ultimately, unworthy of love?

Are the years they tried to cure your disorientation with psychiatric drugs off limits? After all, the fact that you righted yourself, and figured out how to walk, not fly like the obvious gifts your youth once suggested you could do, should be good enough. You are extraordinary not only because you overcame your difficult beginnings, but because you also survived your subsequent lives as Integrator, Fetish, and Exotic Pet. You are like a cat.

How many lives will you cycle through before you have one family who looks at you and understands, who appreciates, what it feels like to walk in this skin? How many masks must you don before you can return to a collective body of love that acknowledges the beauty, the achievement, the shadows, and the strength of Blackness?

You will work to vanquish the voices that tell you they know better. You have overheard their whispers since the day your family brought you home.

-There are good reasons why you've been abandoned.

-Don't forget how lucky you are, not to be dead in a ghetto somewhere, like the girl who gave birth to you.

-They gave you such a good life.

-Beggars can't be choosers.

-Maybe you should press the delete button now and hold it down. Watch it erase the discomfort, bounce over the betrayal, and swallow the recurring sense of loss.

Imagining how things should be can turn off these voices. Write these new realities into being.

Someday your family will make the journey across racial boundaries to visit you in your home. They will stop insisting that if you want to see them, you must always return to face the ghosts that haunt the places of your childhood. Or best of all, your family will stop insisting on living lives far away from Blacks whom they did not raise.

Then, you will visit them in the new places they call home, where there's someone like you on every corner, because they couldn't possibly choose to live somewhere their son, daughter, sister, brother, aunt or uncle—their family—wasn't welcome. They won't abandon politics, either, just because its machinations make them depressed and aware of differences. Nor will they scold you for pointing out that no one talked to nor sat near you and your Black partner at the last family wedding.

The wedding is not about you, and you have no right to ruin it for everyone else.

You must not rage, even when they hurt you. Write that down over and over in your journal, and underline it several times.

They are white. You are Black.

If you ever forget that, your family will remind you. You will be forced to decide which makes you lonelier: your loss of dignity when you are with them or their abandonment of you when you refuse to follow their rules.

They are always in charge, and their needs and comfort come first.

If you ever try to live your life outside of these mandates, their silence will commence. They will try to starve you with it until you give in. Fill that silence and its hunger with writing. But be forewarned; you will sit for a very long time deciding what to say.

MARIETTE WILLIAMS

FENCES

"Good fences make good neighbors"
Robert Frost wrote
Two men each year visit the same spot
To mend a wall
Holding on to tradition, ritual,
Each year repairing the fence
To maintain order, keep the chaos
Away

Good fences make good adoptees
Keep the unknown darkness
Where it belongs
On the other side there are things you don't know
Things that can hurt you
Things that we can't talk about until you are older
When you get older you will understand why we need
Fences

But I tired of the fence
I wanted to know what was on the other side
What was my other side?

I labored over picking out the perfect dress to meet my mother
It was white
A rebirth

We sat beside each other
Our bodies close but the years still between us
At first she hesitated to look at me,

Maybe still not convinced I wasn't a ghost
I spoke to her, my words filtered through a translator
My eyes watching the words hit her ears, dance across her eyes
Then she spoke and I waited for the words to leave the translator's lips
It was jilting, awkward sometimes
I wanted to ask things, say things, confess things
But not to this stranger

I wanted another world where I could open my wounds
That hadn't yet healed
And let her see them
But we smiled for the cameras
I wanted to climb into her skin
And feel what she felt
And see myself in her eyes
And hug and kiss myself with her arms
And mouth

But I could not
I wanted so much more
A lifetime of waiting had left me thirsty for her love

Five days wasn't enough
It wasn't enough to close the gap
To learn everything about the woman who had loved me first

But it still gave me a peace
To see the place where I was born
To know the hour in which I came into the world
Screaming
I wanted so much more
But I got what I needed

When I went home I was asked
"Were your adoptive parents okay with you searching?'
I was 32 years old.

FENCES

Three degrees
Two children
One husband.
"Were they okay with it?"
They ask because they need permission
To climb their own fences
And see what's on the other side

DR. NICHOLAS COOPER-LEWTER

WHO AM I REALLY? IN SEARCH OF HEAVEN ON EARTH

Experience is the language of the Spirit

Henry H. Mitchell

Even God's love must be mediated, long enough, strong enough, and intentionally enough until it can be embraced as real.

Nicholas Cooper-Lewter

OM'S TONGUE TWISTED BY ALCOHOL shouted, "Get out of our house, you black bastard!" In an instant, as if frozen and on fire, I gasped as I grasped a sacred secret. "Being black is in. But Mom, a bastard?" I countered. A man never hits a woman. I was pushed by tiny easily bruised fists backward to the kitchen door and ordered to stand and "don't move!" My mother raced out of the kitchen.

I waited anxiously. My heart pounding, my stomach drawing into a knot, I felt like a person about to be executed. Mother returned, stopped, and stared. Time stopped, then once again her tongue twisted by alcohol in a terrifying and demanding voice screamed, "Here are your walking papers! Get out of my house, you bastard!"

Stumbling out of the door in my house shoes, whose name was on the papers? I recognized on the birth certificate Dad's name and Mom's name. But where was my name? My walking papers? This was "Roots" in real time. Walking papers were needed by slaves to travel. At age 17, in a sweatshirt, jeans, and house shoes where was I expected to travel?

In the space between multiple possibilities, time slowed and my mind outraced my hurt heart and my terrified soul slid into darkness.

Mom showed me her surgical scars when she told the story of how she almost died birthing me in the year 1948. This was an evidence based story; I was skillfully led to embrace as the truth. In the same way, I was repeatedly reminded in this family, I was connected to a long line of difference makers dating back to ancient Kemet with stops along the Anishinabe-Ojibwe, Blackfoot, Seminole, French, Scotch-Irish and German DNA path. I had spent my childhood trying to prove I belonged. Did I just lose it all? Who was I really? My version of heaven on earth dissolved before my weeping eyes and sprinting imagination.

My mind raced to memories from before. Once when traveling to go back to Texas from Minnesota, I watched my 6'3" father drive almost non-stop with only gas and coffee breaks for 12 hours. Once we stopped for coffee to keep Dad awake. The person who sat in the front seat had the job of keeping him awake. At 10, I was given the job. We both started to nod off, which precipitated the unscheduled stop to get coffee before the sun went down. Confused, I watched a giant of a man, my father, bend over and shuffle his way around to the back of the restaurant. I yelled out the window, "Dad, the front door is open, there is a man standing there waiting on you!" "Get him back in the car," he screamed in a scary voice to Mom who had awakened when we stopped. What happened to the powerful big man I called Dad?

Later during that same trip, I went with Mom to town. In a store, I saw two water fountains. One had colored water and the other had white water. At home, I always drank white water. The colored water was warm and rusty looking, so I went to get some white water. An elderly white woman slammed my mouth into the water faucet screaming I had "fouled" all the water. My mother rushed to her, seeing my bloody mouth, and pushed the lady away from me. Grabbing my hand we quickly exited the store. The sun was setting and she mumbled something about getting home before the sun went down. That day I knew who I wanted to be like. I wanted to be a mother like my Mom. She was fearless and protected me. Dad was afraid. I did not want to be like Dad, a father bent over, shuffling, and afraid. What had I now done wrong for Mom to turn on me? Being black meant knowing rules; I must have broken a rule and not known it.

"But Mom, why are you calling me a bastard?" Being a bastard was not good. I had heard certain family members called whores and their children bastards. That could not be me. I had witnessed my Mom's scars and was captivated by the fact that giving me birth nearly killed her. No one had ever told me I was a "bastard." But now, I suspected something was amiss replaying how my siblings were treated so well in comparison. I believed it was the alcohol that sentenced me to weeks and sometimes months of "the silent and invisible" treatment. I blamed alcohol that put me on bread and water for weeks and the need to pay room and board starting at age 15. I made $.25 an hour after school and on weekends working at a supermarket on the bus line that ran in front of the family home.

Home and family was supposed to be "Heaven On Earth." But now not knowing who I really was any more, I feared the unknown, and I realized I needed to find a new heaven on earth. But I needed to find out first who I really was.

Facing an emotional death of who I thought I was, I needed to find the courage to be. But to be what, to be who? I believed we were all basically spirits living and animating a physical body. But being black was more than a body; it was a way of life. Marching on Washington, sitting at the feet of Drs. Clark famous for the "Doll Test" Thurgood Marshall presented to the United States Supreme Court, being the first and often only to integrate all white or nearly all white schools, having a female school friend beaten for calling me a friend. Reminders that being black was not a good thing in the eyes of many did not prepare me for this merger of being "black" and a "bastard" with "walking papers."

I thought about how I had proven my value to my high school football coach in Minnesota. I was the starting quarterback on the freshman squad and third string quarterback on the varsity behind two seniors. I was going to follow in the shoes of my mentor who was dating the "girl" across the alley on the corner. He was the first black quarterback in the Big Ten. Sandy Stephens and all the Golden Gophers were "required" to live in our black zoned neighborhood. We loved seeing and being with these champions and future NFL stars. Some of them even became lawyers and judges.

To my dismay and surprise, Dad took a job in Cleveland, Ohio with the Urban League. The head coach offered to let me stay in Minnesota with him. Coach believed in me. The answer my father gave was, "NO!" Ohio was not as inviting. I was a top student, a city champ in track and field. The school required that I be examined by a school psychologist since I had achieved the impossible. I got perfect scores on their admission tests.

In 1963, we drove to the National Urban League conference in California and caravanned to Washington, DC for the March on Washington. Our family integrated Cleveland Heights, nothing like Saint Paul and Minneapolis. The head coach handed me a lineman's helmet and insisted I play guard. "Coach, I am a great quarterback. I can prove it. Just call my coach in Minnesota." The new head coach said, "No!" I could never prove my worth as a quarterback to him as he dismissed me like a bothersome mosquito. Fortunately, one coach valued me, but I overheard the head coach say he was not risking his job putting a colored kid at quarterback. What would happen seeing a colored kid telling white kids what to do in the suburbs? Being black was not a good thing to be. I lettered in track and football, took honors classes, was intramural wrestling champion, a chess club member, and surprisingly popular. But, being a quarterback, a black quarterback was out of the question.

Then the lady who convinced me I was her baby boy turned on me. Without the aid of alcohol, she was an Omni-competent, beautiful, creative, and compassionate mother. She taught me to sew, cook, shoot baskets, fish, and grow vegetable gardens, write, and speed-read with comprehension.

Later I would learn I was her unmarried sister's second child. Born on my aunt's birthday, the family had decided to keep my roots a secret. Alcohol opened our family's Pandora's Box. I have been traveling ever since.

I continue to search for heaven on earth. Family secrets run deep, I may never know the whole truth. I may need to simply decide who I am so that I can build a heaven where my hells have previously existed. People need to know their story and find out who they are.

Being black continues to be a journey and a quest. You cannot prove anything to anyone no matter how hard you try, especially if they are holding something against you and who you really are.

Experience is the language of the spirit. Even God's love must be mediated, long enough, strong enough, and intentionally enough *until it can be embraced as real.*

JANET PRICE

THE IDENITY GAME

M Y STORY BEGINS WITH BEING born in the early 1950s. My birth mother was 19 and White; my birth father African American and in his mid-twenties. This time in our country's racial history was pre-Martin Luther King, Jr., pre-civil rights. Bad things happened to Black men who consorted with White women. When my White birth mother became pregnant she did not even tell her parents who the father was, assigning her pregnancy instead, not to her secret Black lover, but to her White boyfriend. Before the pregnancy could show, my birth mother was sent away to a Home for Unwed Mothers, where she birthed me, relinquished me to the adoption agency a few days later, and flew back home alone. She arrived back home with a secret that was bigger than anyone knew, except my birth father. He, in the meantime, had left town, possibly to protect him from potentially life threatening repercussions. My birth mother never heard from him again.

I learned later in my life that my adoptive parents had requested a White infant daughter, their first adopted child having been a White infant son. Because my birth mother kept my bi-racial heritage a secret even from the adoption agency, I was placed into this White home "by mistake". As I grew and developed over the coming months, my skin color darkened. Again, I learned much later in life that at that point, as the apparently horrified social workers realized the mistake, they offered my adoptive parents the opportunity to give me back to the agency and start over, this time with a White female infant daughter. One of the proudest moments of my life was learning that my mother responded with a definitive and conscious choosing. She told the social worker that no one could take her daughter away. Unfortunately, I only learned of that experience after my mother died. I was in my twenties.

Growing up as an adoptee brought an added struggle for me about belonging. I was not genetically connected to my parents, or to my siblings. Growing up as a bi-racial adoptee added an additional complexity—I did not look like anyone in my family, or my community, or school. I did not see anyone around me with light-brown skin, kinky brown hair, a space between their front teeth, or a nose shaped like mine. That lack of fundamental connection created much angst, pain, and confusion for me surrounding my identity.

Since I was light-brown skinned, living in an all White family and community, those closest to me chose to interact with me as White. But, I was deeply, though subconsciously, aware of my differences, both biologically and racially. The result was that I struggled to feel grounded and anchored. I can remember an experience in elementary school which highlights the fundamental dilemma of identity that has been, and continues to be, an ongoing thread in the tapestry of my life's narrative.

Everyone in my third-grade class was talking about it—where they came from, who their ancestors were, what made them able to be the proud member of which group. This new awareness of belonging began to surface and take shape for us all, the awareness that each of us has a cultural heritage, something that, once discovered, helps contribute to our growing sense of self. With great excitement, children came to school each day with newly discovered information about themselves: one was half French and half English, another part Irish and part French. I, on the other hand, as an adoptee, felt a desperate need to keep my lack of personal history a secret. I also felt enormous discomfort about telling my classmates that I was adopted. I wondered what I would do, what I would say when it was my turn, as someone else in my circle of classmates seemed to brag about their newly acquired piece of knowledge regarding what connected them to their families, both current and their ancestors. After all, who could provide me with such information? Where did I come from? What culture and country did my ancestors call home?

I found myself squirming. Every day brought on more distress. Classmates continually gathered to share more about what they learned from their parents regarding their biological heritage. What would I do when it was my turn? Would I have to tell them that I was adopted? Would I have to disclose that I did not know anything about my origins?

I already experienced negative reactions in the past from children whom I had shared that I had joined my family through adoption. I naively assumed that everyone would think adoption was a normal way to join a family. I was painfully aware that I would be alone amongst my peers. I knew no other children who were adopted, besides my older brother. The reality was, more than likely, there were others around me who had been adopted. But, like me, such information was kept as secret as possible.

My distress over this "Identity Game" led me to approach my adoptive mother for help.

I explained to my mother what was distressing me at school. I shared with her how I was unsure how to navigate this "Identity Game". My mother's solution was for me to tell my classmates that I was the daughter of an Egyptian princess! Apparently, my mother assumed I was comfortable with my classmates knowing that I was adopted and I simply needed a reply to get me through the situation. She apparently was quite unaware of the underlying pain I was trying to communicate to her, in eight-year-old fashion, the pain and loss of my unknown genetic history and connections. Unfortunately, my mother's suggested solution completely missed the point. What was so excruciating for me, this "Identity Game", was it constantly hammered home to me, in a basic and fundamental way, that I did not know who I was. As I considered my mother's suggested solution I knew, if this story had been true, it would be delightful to share, undoubtedly the best story of all. But, this was not my story, at least as far as I knew.

I tried again, asking my mom for guidance about what to say, if and when it became my turn to share. This time, my mother responded less enthusiastically, reminding me that she knew nothing about my background. I became more aware, again subconsciously, of my mother's discomfort with this conversation and my continued plea for help. This time, my mother announced that I should simply reply as all of the other children did; they were sharing the cultural background of their parents and ancestors, so that is what I should do. My mother was referring, of course, to herself and my father, my adoptive parents. The

47

cultural heritage of my parents who were raising and caring for me each day, were of German and Welsh descent. My mother announced definitively that this could be my response when it was my turn at the "Identity Game" as they were my parents, after all. One of the problems with that suggestion, besides the fact that, again, this was not true, was that I looked nothing like either of my parents, and was aware that I had none of the physical characteristics of the Germans or the Welsh. In fact, many years later I learned what I had already guessed, that I had an African American birth parent (my father). My birth mother happened to be of Irish heritage. Thankfully, my classmates eventually moved on to other areas of shared interest and curiosity without me ever being put on the spot to play the "Identity Game".

These experiences that tapped into my loss at that time were complex. My mother showed me that she was unable to consider or address key aspects of my adoption story with me. Furthermore, she missed my attempt at communicating underlying confusion, rejection, and aloneness. Being the very good adopted daughter I was, I let the topic go and never brought it up with my mother again. At eight years old, as I walked away from the second and final attempt to learn more about myself, I made a commitment to myself. When I grew up, I believed I would adopt. I wanted to give my child what my adoptive mother could not—understanding. I imagined that when my own adopted child asked me about her cultural and biological background, I would lift her up onto my lap, hug her and hold her close. I would tell her that although I do not know anything about her heritage, I understand how it feels to not know. I would give my adopted child, in that moment, what my adoptive mother was not able to give me.

Flash forward 25 years and I was able to carry out the commitment I had made to myself when I was only eight old. After giving birth to two sons, I adopted my infant, bi-racial daughter. What I could not have imagined when I was eight was how profound such an act would be for me, above and beyond what I was able to conceive of at that age. I had thought all that time about the gift I wanted to give to the child I adopted. I could not have imagined how this step would provide such a deep healing for me, as a bi-racial adoptee. My daughter gave me the opportunity to not only love her unconditionally but to also love that part of myself unconditionally. I found myself loving my brown skin as I was amazed at the beauty of her brown skin. I worked towards acceptance of my kinky hair as I celebrated the beauty in her kinky brown hair, seeing these parts of myself that had felt misunderstood and invisible by parents for whom my identity, different from theirs, was foreign and unknown.

Now many years later, I continue my journey of my bi-racial identity. I accept now that I do not fully belong to my Black sisters, nor do I fit in completely with my White friends. I feel some discomfort with Black people, fearing that somehow I will miss a cue that Black women just know, something they learned by being raised by Black mothers who in turn had been raised by Black mothers. It is OK now. It is about being me. It is about the complexity of identity as an adoptee and a bi-racial woman. It is the narrative of being raised by two White parents in the 1950s, who loved me very much and hoped more than anything that I would "pass" and be safe, with doors open to me throughout my life which they assumed would be closed to me if it was known that I was bi-racial.

Though much has changed in the world since that time—more openness about the stories of those connected to the adoption experience, greater understanding about the complexity of adoption, more sensitivity to creating and supporting multi-racial families—we still have a long way to go. Supporting the healthy identity development of a bi-racial adoptee includes love and understanding and acceptance and finding mirrors. It is about supporting the weaving of this experience into the tapestry of our life journey as rich and murky and wonderful and confusing, and OK.

BARBARA ROBERTSON

RECLAIMED HERITAGE

I AM A SAME-RACE ADOPTEE. I have always known that I was adopted. For the first 15 years of my life, I did not think about it much in terms of its impact on my life. I was too busy trying to survive the confusing complexities of a childhood as an only child, dealing with a mother who seemed unhappy in her choice to adopt a person who was very different from her. My father was a gentle, silent man, a hard worker who regularly worked long hours. I knew he loved me, but as time passed, Dad and I rarely spoke except to greet each other or say goodnight. My parents and I would occasionally visit with my adoptive relatives; however, their families were not close. One habit that I had was I would always put "not really" in parentheses in my head when it came to family labels, because I never felt completely like I belonged. I didn't feel connected to others. I always felt like a stranger looking in on a party to which I was not invited.

Every day, I walked in ignorance, not knowing my own origins and had little to inform my future because of it. I had to find my own way and figure how I was going to be in the world for myself. Growing up, I benefited from the post Civil Rights Era of the 60s, the Women's Rights movement of the 70s and my adoptive mother's advocacy for my education. I was able to be enrolled in desegregated schools, getting the opportunity to excel that I unfortunately did not have in the black community at the time. Then I found myself being more obviously an outsider, because I was now in places with people who did not look like me and were also culturally, and economically different. There were many occasions when I was the only or one of a few persons of color. When I was back in my own community, I did not fit in there either. I often felt like I was floating adrift in the middle of an ocean looking out on the horizon, seeing no place to land. To counteract this feeling, I focused on assimilating into society on two fronts, as both a "good black person" and a "good adoptee".

What did that mean to me? It meant that, as a good black person, I had to be smart, educated and successful, (i.e., "a credit to my race"). To paraphrase Dr. Martin Luther King, I would not be defined by "the color of [my] skin, but by the content of [my] character". I heard from an early age that I was given up for adoption so my biological mother could continue her education. I thought that was reasonable, so rather than being angry or sad, I secretly rooted for her. This resonated with me because it meant that she wanted to "be somebody". So did I. This became my driving motivation. I didn't fantasize about her as a famous actress or singer, nor did I create any fairytale about the type of person she was. The most difficult thoughts I had about her was that I didn't know her name, or what she looked like. Because of this, she did not seem "real" to me. Since she was not real, I did not feel real either.

I struggled to remain culturally connected. I remember Black History Month as the time to learn about the contributions of black people. However, I was unaware of how undereducated I actually was about the subject. In addition, like many in my generation, I saw the historic mini-series, "Roots". I was moved by it, but it was nothing more than a story that did not apply to me, for my roots were hidden from me by the legality of closed adoption. I had yet to know the impact of loss I suffered because of not knowing what I didn't know!

As a good adoptee, it meant that I did not talk about adoption to anyone at all. I would never talk about what went on behind closed doors and I would be whatever my adoptive parents (more so my adoptive mom) wanted me to be. I would do what was expected of me. They would never have to regret adopting me because I would always make them proud. This was my mantra for years, justifying my existence, trying to prove myself worthy of being alive. I was adopted seemingly by someone who wanted to mother a girl child initially but then less so with each passing year. I felt like a failure. I entered adulthood determined to not be a mother and damage children. However, when the day came that I found out I was pregnant, it was one of the happiest days of my life. I felt I had been given a chance to be a good mother. My two children, the first blood relatives that I ever knew, taught me that I was capable of loving human beings beyond comprehension. As I look to my children and their potential futures, I have come to realize that my ignorance of my past has affected them too. Adoption is not just about me anymore but about them.

Today, I think about the future of my family and of my race. There is no longer a separation of the two, due to what I have learned since seeing my biological mother's name on a copy of my original birth certificate. I now had a name of a real person! There is a saying that those who do not know history are condemned to repeat it. But likewise there are some things in history that can be wonderful strengths and gifts. Things that can be held onto that will help inform and strengthen the future. I'm now in reunion with my birth mother. My best hope was fulfilled— she managed to survive, make a life for herself and accomplish many things. Yet, to my surprise, she never forgot me. The significance of the missing denied history is even deeper for a black adoptee. Every tidbit of information is so much more precious. I have had conversations with her since about family history, culture and our shared love of learning. When I first met my aunt, she gave me a hug and said "welcome home". My soul healed some more as I sat with her, comfortable in the fact that the two of us were definitely related. It was wonderful telling my uncle how much my sons' achievements mirrored his own. His response, "wow", warmed my heart. After growing up as an only child, I am now a sibling. Getting to know my younger sister has been like a bonus gift that I will always cherish. I felt both the pain of the lost past and the joy of the found present and future where new memories can be made.

So in spite of what adoption took away, I stand here as a witness to the legacy that can be regained and reclaimed. Adoption was not just a one-time event, but it was about the larger issue of separating me from my heritage, my DNA and from who and where I came from. Many families, even today, don't talk about their history because they feel that they are sparing their children the pain of the past. Black ancestors have had to endure some of the most traumatic situations in order to continue to live. They were ripped apart by slavery, and endured many incidences of human cruelty. Yet because they survived, I am here.

Today, I delight in learning about previously unknown Black history, family history—my history. My children and their children will know and be known. I'm glad I can look into someone else's face and see myself reflected back. My world has shifted in ways that I never could've imagined.

I no longer feel as if I'm floating, with no ground under my feet, surrounded by endless waves of water. Now I feel that my feet are firmly planted in human history. I am thankful for being able to reclaim my roots and find out that, as the character, Walter, stated in the play, "A Raisin in the Sun" by Lorraine Hansberry, I "...come from people who had a lot of pride...". These days, I find myself walking a little taller, with my head held higher. The inner storm that used to rage within me has now been quieted, replaced by a greater portion of peace, understanding, acceptance and...

love.

SEAN SPARKS

INTERSECTIONS

ORN, NAMED CHRISTINA, BY A birth mother who spent 2 days
with me in the hospital and then severed her legal relationship
and responsibility for me by signing a voluntary termination
of her parental rights. The unspoken termination waved any rights to
know who she was.

I have acknowledged my identity as a mutant for most of my life.
My identities are the in-between kind, the half of something kind, the
intersection type. I am bi-racial, transracially adopted, culturally Jewish,
light skinned, and transgender.

My parents are the most righteous white parents I know. They
were ahead of the times when I was growing up. We moved to a Black
neighborhood. They surrounded my brother and me with much Blackness. We talked about racism and white supremacy, as well as safety
concerns. My parents fortified our pride and sense of self-worth,
combated bias, walked the talk, modeled our right to ignore the
meddling questions, stares, and affect of surprise and confusion from
others who felt it somehow their right to know how our family who
didn't "match" came to be.

And then we come to the tremors of oppression and powerlessness
that are intertwined in both adoption and the condition of Black
existence.

At 40, I sat with my 76 year old adoptive mother to plan our first
presentation together. Piecing together our conceptualization of the
racial identity development of children of color, who were transracially
adopted (she being white and me being mixed, Irish/Scottish and Black)
had a depth to it, a confirmation of our belonging to each other and
that I am a direct product of my parents' relentless pouring in to me.

We told stories; I listened intently as she broke down and explained her amazing ways of knowing how to support my Black-ness as a white mother.

We explored our perspectives, rooted in theory of folks like Cross, Freire, and Erikson. The conversation moved me, solidified what I have always felt, my white mother understands white supremacy and oppression. My white mother gets how racism, historical and institutional weighs down on her Black children. She lived within the movement, spoke out, interrupted, and shocked her white counter-parts every time she opened her mouth and denounced the ways in which white folks perpetuate sanctioned superiority, complacent in their comfort in white privilege.

My white parents' work directly impacted my development and Black identity in ways that instigated and affirmed my cellular knowing and re-experiencing of a history, woven through contemporary structures, micro-aggressions, invisibility, and emotional self-doubt. My parents' parenting has been the most intimate act of revolution I have ever experienced.

When I give trainings to white folks parenting children of color, I use my parents as a measure of action and awareness although they are a rare representation of and an even rarer reality of what white folks need to do to combat government sanctioned acts against Black bodies, spirits, and minds. I tell them my parents did everything so deeply right in the realm of fortifying my identity and it still was not enough. The reaction to this statement spans the spectrum from gratitude to denial. The denial comes across as such anger toward me for validating their participation in racism and making them uncomfortable in regards to confronting their decision to be oblivious to the reality that their white identity cannot protect their Black children. Their anger often boils over to express the helplessness they feel when they interface with the truth that love is not enough to supply Black children with a substitute for Black love. Not enough to cultivate an identity formation rooted in the love, nuance, and culture that only we can feed and nurture in each other. Those subtle nuances that one can only learn from being grown through Black love in all of its revolutionary forms of survival, community, and a connection that is anchored in our ancestors. Struggle, triumph, and the manifestations of the trauma that silently continues to torture our minds and loudly threatens and steals our bodies through institutions, invisibility, and oppression are pieces of our history that we not only learn from story-telling, but are also validated in our connectedness as real and alive pieces of us.

The generational transmission of our people's experience through our DNA and cellular reproduction as well as interactional patterns that ignite our ability to live rooted in resistance and resilience is awakened through the mirroring and the validation that can only come from one another, from seeing ourselves in the faces of others, beaming with the absolute beauty and LIFE that being Black is.

My white mother and father get this and are not victimized by it. Perhaps that is the most important lesson they taught me about white people's responsibility in the fight.

Through the process of creating our presentation, in the mist of rigorous dialogue and exchange, my mother informs me that there is a story about my adoption that they never told me. I pause; face fills up red and hot, palms sweaty with the mix of excitement and trepidation...

"I never told you because I never wanted it to effect how you felt about yourself," she said. "So what is it? Tell me," I said.

She goes on to tell me and I realize that this is one of the times when it is so painful for my mother to not be able to protect me from racism. She owns it through her words and in the mixture of love and pain on her face.

They got the call about me as a possible "match" and the social worker insisted that my parents meet with her and her supervisor in the office to discuss the particulars. They met with the county workers who explained that my birth mother (who is white) said that my birth father is Black. They continued on to explain that based on my appearance, fair skinned (such a triggering label) white features, that it was hard to believe that I was Black. They hadn't been able to verify my birth father's identity, meaning they couldn't verify that I was Black, which clearly dictated their placement decision.

It hit me with a thud, a knock to my system, a blaring assault on my footing. It flooded like a stream over me. White supremacy dictated my placement with my family while stealing me away from the potential of being with my tribe.

They explained that the county was concerned about placing a white baby with a Black family. In my 40 year old body, my gut immediately went to the thought about their efforts to preserve the white race. I have worked in the adoption field for over ten years. I believe there is an undeniable and unspoken rule that state adoption agencies and the county do not endorse white children being adopted by folks of color.

That moment exploded inside of my spirit, my internal locus of control was knocked off its axis. I was refused placement with a Black family because white supremacy dictated who my family would be just as it would have dictated my placement on the plantation, just like it dictates my mobility as a professional, just as it dictated the perceptions of me throughout my educational life, just as it has served to separate me from Black folks.

Racism stole from me my right to be raised by my people. The trauma that is stored in my DNA screamed, seeped out through the cracks, and sent me to an ugly place in which I was separate, in a space between and in that place I had to accept that racism had taken something else from me.

My parents rallied their friends and discussed this situation. The final decision was that at worst, they would be raising a white child to be informed and influenced by people of color.

Upon my arrival to my new family this same group of friends, who it is important to state are Black, took one look at me and immediately claimed my Blackness for me, rooted in my cuticles, a racial identification tool that is another symptom of the history of racism, murder, and slavery that on this occasion, worked to identify me.

As days passed, all kinds of feelings ran over me. A sadness grew in my gut, some strange sense of loss crept into my spirit.

I realize now that this has a deeper meaning than simply a missing piece of my story finally delivered 40 years later. The depth is this. From a couple days old until I joined my family I was with a foster mother. She sent me home with clothing and my favorite stuffed bunny. She shared about my routines and temperament, likes and dislikes with my parents. I was healthy and my spirit vibrated that I had been loved. This was another loss for my infant self, another trauma, disconnected attachment.

My inner dialogue began. They wouldn't have let her keep me. She was Black and I was too light to be adopted by a Black woman. White supremacy robbed me of her. Racism simplified her role in my life as an extension of the Black mammy. She kept a white woman's child, loved and cared for me in ways my own birth mother couldn't or wouldn't. The state in all their suppression of Black life and love and dedication to white supremacy dictated that racism again would rip me from my people.

That next layer, that adoption, is also a system of oppression and power, that race, privilege, and resource gives white folks access to children of color with few barriers is certainly a reflection of institutional racism as it is another intersection of systems that work against our preservation and serves an unspoken purpose. Children of color make up the majority of those in the child welfare system in my state and Black children are removed from their parents at disproportionate numbers.

The power inherent in adoption has shown me—adoptive parents and biological parents can hold our stories, our truth, our beginnings, and can also keep our people away from us if they chose. I don't believe there is another system where lying through omission is endorsed as it is in criminal prosecution, incarceration, racism, and adoption. A system designed to take us from our families and farm us out to white folks to be raised to be one standard deviation away from who we were created to be, Black.

Our stories are our stories no matter the difficulty we feel in living in our truth. Loss in adoption hurts and shifts our understanding of relationships forever. Loss through racism can equate to death. Our systems retain our implicit and non-verbal memories. We remember. We cannot fully integrate without the language of our stories.

My biological father is Black. He found me 2 years ago and for the first time, I saw myself mirrored in someone else's face. Although affirming, I had always known I was Black and this was affirmed by other Black folks in interactions and introductions that may to them have seemed unimportant but to me were a series of verbal affirmations that they claimed me.

We are surrounded by tangible evidence of state sanctioned violence. Recently—with the continued lynching of Black people by police officers, the growth of the Black Lives Matter movement, and the reactions of some to the pressures of police brutality and murder, it is vitally important we as a people deconstruct how white supremacy visits itself in our multiple identities. In my opinion—the adoption/foster care system are institutions complicit with a system built on white supremacy and works tirelessly to systemically drive Black people to a continued loss of connection to each other.

LIZ SEMONS

SOME OF US REALLY ARE ALONE

Y NAME IS LIZ SEMONS and I am a black and white transracial adoptee who was born in 1968. I was adopted by a Caucasian family and moved to a suburb of San Francisco bay area CA at the young age of six. Let me just say...I was the only girl in school rocking an afro. Funny now but then...not so much! I started off color blind but it did not last long as the mirror does not lie. I felt different, ugly and insecure. I just never felt a sense of belonging as I only had a brother who was also adopted and just as confused as I was. He also was black. This did help some but not enough to secure my shaky ground. When he was not around, there was nobody around that looked like me.

When divorce struck our family, my brother and I were sent to boarding schools as my adopted parents were ready to move on with their lives. I was sent to boarding school at the age of fifteen. My adopted brother was sent to a school in Ohio and I was sent to one in Nevada City, CA. The school was in the middle of nowhere and full of hippies. At this point, I found myself even more confused about who I was and why I was unwanted. I now felt rejected not only once but twice.

Needless to say it was a very confusing time for me. At my boarding school there were a few other black kids but only three including me. Still, I was happy to see them. Just knowing that I was not the only one was a huge relief!

Luckily at this school I met another adoptee who I became very close with. We lost contact after we were expelled from our school due to our wild behavior. The school I attended really was like a party that lasted a year. There was nobody watching our every move and most of the kids there were partying quite a bit. It almost felt like I had started college about four years too soon.

Although I was starting to have fun with kids my own age for the

61

first time, it was not the way a fifteen year girl old should have been living. Our wild behavior consisted mostly of hitchhiking, shoplifting and underage drinking. The shoplifting began only because we were not receiving any finances from anyone. I know that is not an excuse but it was our reality. Thank God those days are over!

Twenty-six years went by after my friend and I were expelled for staying out late and coming back to campus extremely intoxicated. I stayed with my adopted father for a little while after this but my friend and I were not allowed to see each other for a time. Soon I was on my own. I worked and rented rooms and even had to drop out of school to keep my head above water.

In 2011, out of the blue, I received an email from my long lost friend Denise from boarding school. She saw a post that I had done many years prior on an adoption search website. I almost did not open the email as I did not recognize her name as it had changed since she was now married. I am so glad that I did not delete it as it was the best email that I have received in all my years!

Denise started to ask me all that I knew about my adoption and I told her everything!

To my biggest surprise, two months later, I was talking to my biological mother on the phone. My friend was able to use the information I knew and the skills she had learned. She found my family! I have never been so amazed in all my life.

It is true what they say about dear friends. Denise and I reunited after twenty-six years. It was as if no time had passed at all. I could not believe what was happening. Not only was I reuniting with my best friend from many moons ago... she was sitting on the plane next to me. We were flying together to Ohio to meet my mother Joanne for the first time. Now that is a reunion.

After this journey I did not know what to do. I was so excited and also in shock. I had so much I needed to get out. I started to write and write. I have been plucking away at my memoir called "Strength of the Broken" which has been written and re-written many times. I hope soon I will feel it is just where I want it. I am learning that writing a book is not easy. I just hope to keep readers wanting to turn the page. I am determined to get there. I also have written many adoption songs. I have submitted my newest project called "Knock at your door" which is a reunion song and one that I am amazed to this day that I was able to write. I hope that many more adoptees have the opportunity to knock at that door and to look in those eyes. Keep trying and keep believing. What I truly realize now is that miracles can and do happen! –Liz Semons

Lyrics: "Knock at your Door" Written By: Liz Semons © 2016 (Adoption Reunion Song)

Knock at your door
Knock at your door
Knock at your door
Knock at your door…

To knock at your door
To knock at your door
Is what I've prayed for…

To knock at your door
To knock at your door
Is what I've hoped for
To knock at your door…

I can't wait…
To knock at your door
Knock at your door…
Can't wait…
To knock at your door…
Knock at your door

To look in your eyes
To look in your eyes
Is what I dreamed for
To look in your eyes…
To look in your eyes

To look in your eyes
Is what I've lived for
To look in your eyes.

I can't wait
To look in your eyes
Look in your eyes
Can't wait
To look in your eyes...

Time
It's my first time
To knock at your door
Time
It's my first time
To look in your eyes.

Lost without you
Lost without you
I was lost without you
Lost without you
Lost without you
Lost without you
But dreams come true
Lost without you

I can't wait...
To knock at your door
Knock at your door
Can't wait...
To look in your eyes

APRIL DINWOODIE

ATTENTION ADOPTIVE PARENTS: HAVE YOU EVER STARTED A CONVERSATION ABOUT RACE?

WHAT I AM REALLY ASKING is...have you ever started a conversation about differences of race, class and culture in order to better understand yourself, your children and the world we live in?

If you parent a child that is a different race than you, I hope you have. If you adopted the child you are parenting that is a different race than you, I really hope you have. If you have not, I find myself angry, confused and heartbroken for you and for your extended family, but mostly for your child.

Let me be clear, even if you are not parenting a child of another race, if you are simply living in the world in 2016, I hope you too have started a conversation about race at least once in your life. Let me be even clearer, if you are an adoptive parent and your child is a different race than you, it is imperative that you have not only started conversations about differences of race, class and culture, but that you are doing so openly, honestly, authentically and often. These conversations are a critical part of your overall efforts in support of your children and your multicultural family. This important, additional work is imperative for your child's healthy identity development and ultimately their safety in the world both emotional and physical.

As a person of color adopted by a white family, I can say that it is not only necessary but urgent that parents and professionals are talking openly, honestly, authentically and often-about differences of race, class and culture, and realizing that while a key ingredient to raising children, love is really not enough. Similarly, the notion of being color blind is as unrealistic as it is unhealthy for positive identity development. We are not, nor should we ever be, blind to any aspect of what makes a person who they are. Their race, their ethnicity, their culture of origin and experience are essential aspects of any human being.

"During the time she was in the foster home, baby was seen ten times by the agency pediatrician. She was also seen by a geneticist who gave the opinion that it was possible the baby was of mixed race." "Because you had a Mongolian spot on your buttocks which can indicate Mediterranean or Black heritage, you were seen by a geneticist who gave the opinion that it was possible you were biracial." Both of these statements come from my non-identifying information obtained in my twenties. From the very beginning of my adoption experience differences of race were benign "possibilities"; they were after-thoughts, a professional's opinion but seemingly not something anyone needed to concern themselves with and only something that you could kind of "see" if you really wanted to, if you were *really* looking.

In essence, I think the agency in their efforts to close my adoption, closed off any opportunity for a real dialogue about my race. With children of color often labeled "hard to place," making light of race made it easier and quicker. The thinking was getting parents closer to a "yes" was better for everyone. In word and action, the agency made it OK not to have conversations about race. That would be easier for everyone. Everyone, of course, but me. What this felt like more often than not was that the color of my skin was an afterthought. The "nappyness" of my hair was an afterthought. My physical features were an afterthought, if they were thought about at all.

It was never an afterthought for me and I don't think it ever will be.

I am proud to be a woman of color and I want people to see my brown skin and curly brown hair. I want to have conversations about race. I need to have conversations about race. It is not OK to gloss over these differences anymore and allow only some professionals who transact transracial adoption to do all they can to prepare parents, while others do little or nothing. All of the little black and brown boys and girls need their parents and the professionals that serve them to talk about race, to understand their own inherent biases and prejudges and to act in transformational ways surrounding differences of race, class and culture.

The world is getting far more complicated and yes, love is a key ingredient but loving your children means that you are digging deep within yourselves. Digging deep to embrace your child's full identity and family of origin whenever possible. Digging deep until you are uncomfortable. Digging deep so you can do everything in your power to gain information about your child's biological roots and culture. Digging deep to understand you may never truly understand what it means to be a person of color if you aren't one. And being confident that when you do all of these things, you still need to occasionally do the unthinkable—admit you don't know what to do or how to fix something so complicated, but still do the work necessary to fiercely love and protect your child of color. And then, hold them, weep with them, be angry with them, be confused with them and be heartbroken with them.

We need to really see a child to show them love; and when we see them, we have to see all parts of what make them who they are. We have to celebrate all parts that make them who they are so when they look in the mirror they love what they see. The entire family must own and embrace all of these parts and their transcultural identity. This process starts with a very important conversation and it is a transformational dialogue that will continue over the course of a lifetime. We do all these things for our children to show them how much we love them. We do all these things so our children can love themselves.

JOSHUA CROME

A JOURNEY TOWARDS KNOWING

I WAS BORN IN CHICAGO ILLINOIS' Near West Side, not far from the United Center where my beloved Bulls and Blackhawks play. What I knew of my parents was not very much: My mother was of Norwegian and Irish stock, and looked a lot like Mary Travers. I was told my father was biracial... I knew nothing else about him. Both of my parents were young. That's about all I knew. My adoptive parents were likely told that I was ¼ black because I was so fair-skinned... it probably helped my marketability.

I was adopted into a white progressive Chicago family who tried to make sure that I knew at least something about my background. I grew up having a dashiki in my wardrobe along with my Notre Dame mini varsity sweater. Dr. King, the Freedom Riders, and the Woolworth's lunch counter sit-in activists were revered figures. We watched Jesse Jackson's speech to the Democratic National Convention in 1988 and were amazed at the moment (though I was a Bush-Quayle guy in a house full of Dukakis-Bentsen people!). I had siblings who were black, white, and transracial. We joked that our family resemblance was that we had none. Race was ever present, as a very nontraditional-looking family we did worry about going certain places, but the Rainbow Family concept was something that we wanted to emulate.

When at the age of forty I began searching for my natural/biological family, I had no idea where to begin or what and who I'd find. Eventually I happened upon the State of Illinois' website where I could register in IARMIE—the Illinois Adoption Registry and Medical Information Exchange. Surely this would get me closer to my goal- but it did not. I found out that I could write the state for my non-identifying information from my file. I received a one-page letter that told me some of what I knew: My mom was 18 and my dad was 20 at the time of my birth. A bit later, I was able to apply for a non-certified copy of my original birth certificate or OBC. I waited six long months for my OBC and a year later was able to locate my mother. I am a lot like Mom—left-handed, a bit artsy, a foodie, and a fan of Chicago and Wisconsin, where her side of the family is from. We were able to trace branches of the family tree back to the young man who emigrated from Norway in 1881.

Two years later, I was able to reunite with my father and my uncle. I found out so much more information about my family that I'm still sorting through it all and yet hungering for more. I was so much like Mom that I was absolutely floored when I found out how much like Dad and my uncle I am: I look a lot like him, we're both near-sighted, love fast food (Portillo's!), and we are both car guys. One of my brothers (Mom's sons from her subsequent marriage) remarked how my father and I have the same penchant for funny sayings,

"Josh-isms" in my case.

On my dad's side we are from Florence, Alabama—the family migrated to Cincinnati and then to the Chicago area. In addition to being African-American, we have Creole, French, and Cherokee in our family. We have some roots in New Orleans and ancestors who came from Martinique! Even though I fancy myself a decent student of geography but I had to look up exactly where Martinique was in the Caribbean! No wonder I enjoyed my visits to New Orleans as a kid. So I am actually one-half Black, "Black" encompassing all the admixtures that so many African-Americans have. There's so much more complexity than a simple sentence on adoption paperwork admits. I wish I'd have had known sooner, but I'm incredibly lucky to be where I'm at now.

I am simultaneously worried and encouraged at what I see when I look out at the landscape. I'm worried because I turn on the TV or look at the news online and I see racial animus and discord the likes of which we have not seen in America since the 1960s. It feels at times that this nation is coming apart at the seams, and one of the main fissures is race. People have said things in my presence that are really ugly. I sometimes get a glimpse into some things that seem reminiscent of the old "Saturday Night Live" sketch where Eddie Murphy disguises himself as white and gets cocktails and hors d'oeuvres on the city bus after the last Black person departs it. I've seen evil directed at me and my family by people whose own ancestors just a mere century ago would have been termed undesirable. I am heartened however by seeing that race and color do not have to be barriers to friendship, love, and family. This is possible on a macro level because I see it every day on a micro level with family, friends, and colleagues who treat each other the way they would like to be treated. I hope that our better angels can prevail.

TARA LINH LEAMAN, JD

H.A.N.A.I*

The 3" x 2" wrinkled photo has tattered corners and a yellow stain on its left side. It shows a Black, Asian two-year-old with knobby knees, a head full of curls and dark brown eyes. A small sign in front of her reads "Ho Thi Linh Chi #42". The photographer snapped this image at a time and place when such orphan babies had little chance of survival.

F OR AS LONG AS I can remember, I have carried that photo in my wallet so that I do not forget where I come from. I was born in a small hamlet ninety kilometers from Hue in central Vietnam, the child of a Vietnamese villager and an African American soldier. Soon after I was born, my birth mother placed me on the steps of an orphanage in Hue. Two years later, two pacifists from Pennsylvania adopted me. My adoptive parents, Swiss German American Mennonites who practiced medicine, raised me on a farm in Lancaster County, PA. I spent my childhood driving a tractor, baling alfalfa and cleaning out sheep and horse stalls. I lived in a home where the Mennonite-based commitment to social justice and community was taken seriously. Our family spent summers volunteering at schools for deaf children in Kingston, Jamaica, assisting medical missions in Central America and renovating trailer park homes in Harlan County, Kentucky.

My parents taught me to view the law not as an instrument of justice, but as a tool of manipulation. They believed the law created more problems than it solved. During my high school Civics 101 class discussion of the Civil Rights Act of 1964, I came to realize that the law could protect me, harm me or do both, and in ways which my white parents would never experience. Because some of my peers called me a "nigger orphan" and "faggot Alabama porch monkey," I then understood that I lacked the privilege of distancing myself from the law. The politics of inclusion and exclusion have marked my identity since.

At nineteen I traveled to Africa to claim the most physically apparent aspect of my identity, my African ancestry. Since then, living and working in Africa, Asia, and Latin America, I have discovered that, because of my background, I can move in and out of quite distinct cultures, frequently acting as the interpreter between them. As an adult, I recognize that I do not need to identify myself as just an adoptee, just an African American, just a Vietnamese American or just a lesbian. Instead, I find myself being the bridge between chosen myriad identities. In my effort to negotiate and navigate a life's journey that recognizes and honors the burden and dignity of difference, I have closely held onto the tradition of "Hanai", as described in Dr. Joyce McGuire Pavao's seminal work, The Family of Adoption.

Hanai, as highlighted by Dr. Pavao, is a Hawaiian belief that the adopted child is the bridge between different families, cultures and communities. As I interpret Hanai, I believe it offers 5 key ingredients that lead to an individual's and community's success, especially those of us who are intimate members of the adoption-foster care constellations. "H" is for Healing. "A" is for Anchors. "N" is for Nurture/Nature. "A" is for Adopt/Adapt. And "I" is for Interdependence. H.A.N.A.I.

"H" is for Healing…with the support of family, friends and comrades, I continue to learn that Healing may not necessarily mean knowing the answers, but continuing to ask the questions—within, with and without fear of ambiguity and/or vulnerability…***Healing.***

"A" is for Anchors…that both lift me up and, at times, weigh me down. "Tara ain't really Black, Tara ain't really Asian, you know her parents are white, right, or "She's Black but you can't really tell because she articulate and clean." Sentiments that have affirmed my choice to claim my African heritage first and foremost because of the reality that Whites and Asians have not always welcomed me into their communities. Continental Africans and African Americans, always and, yes, with questions too, but without the pre-conceived judgments. Words that wound that weigh me down balanced with feelings of affirmations that keep me lifted…***Anchors.***

"N" is for Nurture...How do we choose to nurture our nature? And how do we choose the nature of nurturing others? How do we find the joys while incessantly navigating and negotiating the pain of profound losses within ourselves, each other and in our communities? How do we expose each other to realistic, positive and resilient images of each other, and our cultures and communities? How do we advance social justice, equality and equity in a world that often views us as less than? *Nurture and Nature.*

"A" is for Adapt...AdApT: AdOpt. We have all come from so much, but know so little. AdApt. AdOpt. Only 1-vowel distinguishes the two... *AdApt. AdOpt.*

"I" is for Interdependence...to counter the myth that one can be truly independent. We all need each other, and for those of us belonging to the constellation of adoption and/or foster care, our existence is that which blends two or more families, birth and chosen, to make ourselves whole. *Interdependence.*

As I continue to build bridges between my personal background and professional experiences, I anticipate strengthening my ability to listen, share, learn, and unlearn, from and with others through the Powers of Ambiguity, Vulnerability and H.A.N.A.I.

On April 4, 2001, I visited the building that I thought the war had destroyed. While standing in the courtyard of Ly Bang orphanage facing the same wall that I squatted next to as a two-year-old, I studied my toddler photo. I already knew the spirits of my birth relatives lived within me so I had not returned to search for more tangible birthroots. I had returned to discover the part of my ancestry that is more easily disguised, and to learn more about a society that was in the midst of its own human rights stirrings. On the same trip, I traveled with a Vietnamese friend to meet her family who lived in a hamlet located in the heart of the Mekong River Delta. My friend's eighty-years-young grandmother looked me in the eyes and whispered, "You are Vietnamese". In that moment, I became fully aware of where I came from, so much of what I had lost and gained and, most importantly, how much I had yet to learn.

*This piece accompanies a documentary entitled *"Operation Babylift"* that premiered at the NYU Cantor Film Center in Fall 2010. *Operation Babylift* offers a visual narrative of the controversial $2 million U.S. initiative that airlifted over 2,500 Vietnamese orphans in 1975, and features the writer. In addition, this writing sample is an excerpt from a draft memoir entitled, So What Part of Africa is Vietnam In?

CHRISTOPHER WILSON

YOU HAVE HIS EYES

I saw a vision a long long time ago
He sat there perched on a rowing boat.
He spoke soft yet stern
of things that were and weren't there.
I've waited for you longer then you'd fathom to know.
Sitting there face to face.
I am you
His words displaced my own self.
And all I can think with no language to speak
as He looks back at me
my frame frozen in his stare
is who am I to you this man from thin air.
A fainted whisper through sealed lips dissipates the lie
sulking there idly by biding his own time
whispered to me is the truth you have His eyes.

I saw my life pass by me in the stars.
He laughed a jovial boast from his belly.
The bearded man in the sky
I saw him there pass me by
His touch released all my fears
a well spring came of flowing tears
streams of living water burst
springed at the source
by the lending of His voice.

I gazed into these lands on a ninth dimension.
He spoke soft and stern to me.

An aura that commanded respect
He reached down humbly with His right hand
and placed it gently on my flesh
I am you He said.
A caveman who'd been unhinged
can I go back and get my friends?
He laughed and said in His own words
this view is only for you.
I've crossed the line I've drawn in the sand
and now for us there is no separation.
Speaking He looked then right at me
and whispered words passed by my ear
you have His eyes.
They floated by and caught a ride with the notion I surmised.
You have His eyes.
And yet still He pleaded
my son I so deeply needed
to see you know
before I send you the way home.

He spoke soft and stern to me.
Asleep to what was there I came down and went looking in secret.
Discreetly I was peaking.
And now I'll make myself known to thee.
The apple does not fall far from the tree.
My theatrics made you scared
yet all of this was so you can be prepared to sit in this space with me
rowing along merrily.
I shook you loose to let you go
and bring you back in my control.

The waves began to rock.
The boat swayed against the docks.
His eyes pierced right through me as he spoke soft yet sternly.
It's time for us to go.
To the things written on a scroll...

Nodding my head gazed at the planks below.

He beheld me in His arms.

As if to say for so long I needed to let you know that you have His eyes.

Spoken to the percussion of the boats row.

You have His eyes.

He soft yet sternly speaks a whisper.

Told to the one He called his son before the earth had spun and time again begun.

AMANDINE GAY

WHO'S CLAIMING US?

"**B**ounty", "Oreo", you know the drill, wherever we're from those same ol' tired, sweet and sour culinary metaphors are here to remind us that our claiming of Blackness won't necessary be met by the welcoming arms of our people. And yet, I've chosen to be Black. Not in some messed up Dolezal, attention seeking, appropriative way but in a healing, empowering road to (re)discover my roots. I look Black (even if I'm probably mixed Arab/Black), and this is why, growing up in France, I've always been categorized as such, way before I chose to (re)claim my Blackness.

First day in my new school, I'm 5 years old, it's time to line up to get inside the class, I approach one of my classmates (in an almost entirely white school where most of the children of color were adopted by the way) and here it comes: "I'm not holding your hand, you're Black." Two major pieces of information were brutally delivered to me that day: a) I was Black and b) it was reason enough for other children to refuse to hold my hand. My heart was broken, not only because of rejection but also because this incident marked the beginning of what would become my regular disappointments at my parents' helplessness.

My parents: two endearing white middle-class French people who fought their way out of the working-class. Mom saw and used the, then efficient, French meritocratic educational system that not only made her the first woman of her family to attend high school and then college, but also allowed her to become a teacher. Dad quit school at 14 and started working as a locksmith in a factory and quickly managed to oversee construction projects. A most unusual couple in rural France in the 1970s with an atheist worker married to a Christian teacher who was making more money than him. And when they realized that my dad could not have children, contrary to most people who first try ART, they went straight to domestic adoption because my mom has always had pretty hard feelings towards transnational adoption. Long before people started to question it, she considered this practice to be unethical (if not un-Christian). In her view: how could one involve money in adoption? Once they were grown up, what would these children say about the fact that you took them away from their country?

And yet, being as French as it comes, race never entered her/their critical thinking on adoption. To be fair, their multiracial family was some kind of an "accident". My parents had been on the domestic adoption waiting list for quite a while when my mom met my brother in her class (he was placed in a group home at the time). My brother was a great kid who was never visited by his biological family so, knowing that my parents were on the adoption waiting list, a social worker offered for them to start mentoring him: he would spend week-ends and holidays with my parents. Their relationship went on like this for a while, more than a year actually and thus, the status of limitation for parental custody had expired for my brother's first family (the French law states that after a year without any visits from your biological family, you can be adopted). The social worker then suggested that my parents filed for custody and since my brother was happy with it, they did.

As it turns out, my brother was Black. In the 1980s, "rainbow families" were NOT a thing in rural France and when the social services heard about the upcoming birth of a little girl whose Moroccan mother insisted on pointing out that she would be Black, they called my parents. If they were ok with adopting another child of color, they would not have to wait another four years to expand their family. And that is how my parents went from temporary mentors to parents of two Black kids. So, now that I'm also an adult, I see how unfair it is to put them in the same basket as the White "Cumbaya" singing hippies with no perspective on race of their era just because they adopted two Black children in an all-white French village in the 1980s. In their case, it sort of "happened", they were definitely naive, but at least they had not been fetichisizing or performing their dream of a colorblind society through us. They were just truly colorblind themselves, utterly oblivious to racial discrimination because, in their experience, race was indeed, not an issue.

So, back to my first disappointment: here I am, standing like an idiot in the middle of the schoolyard, surrounded by little white kids who are asking why my mom (who teaches in the school) is White. And it hits me, I look at my arm, I look at theirs and suddenly, I see it too. I'm Black, actually, I see myself as brown, which I tell them but they all agree: I'm Black. And I feel betrayed: how could my parents tell me that I'm adopted from such an early age that I don't even remember being told and leave out such an enormous piece of information?!! How could they not see that I was Black? Were they that stupid? And if they saw and did not tell me, why were they so mean? Why leave me to be ridiculed in a schoolyard when it was so easy to notify me that I was different?

That feeling of helplessness and betrayal characterized my childhood and crystallized a very deep resentment of my parents. I later confronted them about their (much too late) realization that racism was alive and well. My mom argued that at the time she truly believed that my brother's reports were exaggerated, and I now believe her. She just could not see it. After all, she came from a poor family and the French republican system had worked for her, it was designed to even inequalities of birth. If the educational system was not discriminating along class lines, why would it discriminate along race lines? So we grew up being torn apart by white supremacy while my parents were watching or should I say looking the other way, offering all sorts of irrelevant comments on how me and my brother were not really being discriminated against. And yet, it was happening all the time, pretty much everywhere we went, including my grandparents' house. Oh the jokes about my hair, oh my grandpa's refusal to sit me on his lap on the grounds that I was "too big" compared to my white cousin (we were the same age) and so forth and so on.

Long story short, I've always been a tough cookie and this hatred fueled my desire to take over the world, which I did (I'm not done yet, but I foresee world domination for 2028). Sadly for my brother and all the other transracial adoptees in my school, the outcome was not so "positive" (I could write another essay on the overachieving transracial adoptee syndrome and its damaging psychological effects, but not today). And this is why this issue has to be politicized: it is unfair and unethical to leave all my brothers and sisters in relinquishment's destiny to fate. You're a tough cookie, you might stay alive and sane enough to pursue a decent life, you're a sweet cookie, too bad, you'll be eaten alive, better luck next time! I cannot accept that, I want all of us cookies to make it to adulthood, and I do not mean in a capitalist and utilitarian perspective of "what those kids could bring to the world". I mean, us, being here, is enough. And our people as in, the global Black diaspora, not just black transracial adoptees, should claim us.

I discovered the 1972 statement on interracial adoption by the *National Association of Black Social Workers* (NABSW), in my mid-twenties:

> The National Association of Black Social Workers has taken a vehement stand against the placement of black children in white homes for any reason [...] The socialization process for every child begins at birth and includes his cultural heritage as an important segment of the process. In our society, the developmental needs of Black children are significantly different from those of white children. Black children are taught, from an early age, highly sophisticated coping techniques to deal with racist practices perpetrated by individuals and institutions. These coping techniques become successfully integrated into ego functions and can be incorporated only through the process of developing positive identification with significant black others. Only a black family can transmit the emotional and sensitive subtleties of perception and reaction essential for a black child's survival in a racist society. Our society is distinctly black or white and characterized by white racism at every level. We repudiate the fallacious and fantasied reasoning of some that whites adopting black children will alter that basic character.[1]

I felt betrayed again, but this time by my people. How come these

1 National Association of Black Social Workers. (1972). Position Statement on Transracial Adoption. *The Adoption History Project*. [Base de données]. Récupéré de http://pages.uoregon.edu/adoption/archive/NabswTRA.htm

struggles never made it to the francophone Black communities? How come nobody was claiming us? Little people have no agency, so if Black communities don't stand up to protect us, who will? And then it hit me: as exemplified by my parents, race was absent from public and scholarly debate when I grew up, and it has only made a comeback due to violent episodes in the recent past.[2] In this context French Black communities, contrary to the Black British or the African American communities are mostly abiding by this informal law that states that advocating for Black people's rights is somehow racist because you can either be French or Black, Black French not being an option.

Race is such a taboo in France that an amendment to the Constitution[3] was passed in 2013 to ban the word "race" from it. Ethnic statistics are forbidden on the account that they are... racists! And as far as slavery and colonialism are concerned, it is a constant struggle to not have these memories erased. In 2005, the article 4 of a law concerning the history connecting France's former colonizers to its colonized populations proposed to introduce a passage in educational textbooks that would present the "positive aspects" of colonization.[4] In 2015, the Administrative Court in Guadeloupe[5] (French West Indies) ruled in favor of a Guadeloupian lobby (read slave-owner descendants)

2   Gay, A. (2015). Deny and Punish: A French History of Concealed Violence. *Occasion*, (9).
http://arcade.stanford.edu/sites/default/files/article_pdfs/Occasion_v09_gay_final.pdf

3   Stille, A. (2014). Can The French Talk About Race? *The New Yorker*.
http://www.newyorker.com/news/news-desk/can-the-french-talk-about-race

4   Loi n° 2005-158 du 23 février 2005 portant reconnaissance de la Nation et contribution nationale en faveur des Français rapatriés.
http://legifrance.gouv.fr/affichTexte.do?cidTexte=JORFTEXT000000444898

5   (2015). La justice autorise une stèle faisant « l'apologie du colonialisme » à Ste Rose (Guadeloupe) [Justice authorizes a stele advocating colonialism in Ste Rose (Guadeloupe)]. *Seneweb*.
http://www.senenews.com/2015/03/12/la-justice-autorise-une-stele-faisant-lapologie-du-colonialisme-a-ste-rose-guadeloupe_117108.html

who wanted to erect a monument in honor of the first French colonizers (read murderers of indigenous peoples who then implemented slavery). The proud people of Guadeloupe immediately destroyed it[6] but this is telling enough of the constant state of disdain and erasure that Black people face in France. In a nutshell, in my country "race" is a word not to be uttered and political institutions as well as most scholars avoid recalling the existence and implementation of a biological and political racism that started as early as the 16th century (the first French slave ship left in 1594).

This erasure of Black people's history and specific existence combined to the universal republicanism rhetoric plays a role in the difficult politicization of adoption. For example, my scholar and activist work focuses on France's history of social engineering as a tool to understand how transnational and/or transracial adoption is a phenomenon still deeply embedded in the colonial continuum. Therefore, I am both going against the idea of a "one and undividable Republic" and against the "positive outcomes" of colonization narrative. And yet, I won't stop until every little cookie knows that there are now more and more former little cookies looking out for them.

The gratitude narrative has to go, whether regarding colonization or adoption. If anybody should be grateful, it's adoptive parents and by association France. Transnational and/or transracial adoption is a rational process, the "right to children" and the "love conquers all" narratives too often mask that (a vast majority) of white prospective parents from the global North do not start their parenting project with a plan to adopt children of color. Did you know that in France transracial and/or transnational adoption is the second if not fifth choice of parenting? 75% of French candidates[7] to adoption first try biological

---

6   N.D. (2015). La stèle en mémoire des « colons » détruite [The monument in honour of the first « colonizers » destroyed]. *France-Antilles*. http://www.guadeloupe.franceantilles.mobi/actualite/societe/la-stele-en-memoire-des-colons-detruite-315297.php

7   Halifax, J., Villeneuve-Gokalp, C. (2005). *L'adoption en France : qui sont les adoptés, qui sont les adoptants ?* [Adoption in France : who is adopting, who are the adoptees ?]. https://www.ined.fr/fichier/s_rubrique/18712/pop.et.soc.francais.417.fr.pdf

procreation then when it fails, they turn to ART, when this fails, they file for domestic adoption. And only then, when confronted to the domestic adoptions' waiting list issue, they consider transnational adoption. This is usually when they find out about the shortage of "white babies" and start considering transracial adoption. And just like with race, if they are oblivious to the fact that we are their second to fifth choice, we are not. So we are not grateful, because we know exactly which purpose we serve. For every "child in need" there are prospective adoptive parents indeed.

This is what I vow to bring to light in the upcoming years in France and more generally the francophone global North: transracial and transnational adoption is a highly political issue rooted in colonialism, capitalism and patriarchy. And this will be my way to claim my own, my Black brothers and sisters in relinquishment and let them know that they are proud and loved members of the Black diaspora.

CATANA TULLY

WHAT IF WE CHOSE OUR LIFE, AND OUR OBSTACLES TURN OUT TO BE BLESSINGS?

AT SOME POINT WE ALL question the purpose of being alive. Why am I here? We wonder. What is being alive about? How do I fit in the world, in my society? Who am I? Particularly the last question figures prominently in the minds of adoptees. Those of us who have dark skin and grew up as an "exotic" child in the White world grapple with much confusion; the sort of confusion we, more often than not, are fearful to address. Worse, we might be ashamed of a problem we think we created by having lost that 'protective coating' we believe our birth parents would have given us.

For a long time I believed my confusion about who I was and how I fit in the world lay in having been a dark child adopted into a White family. When time came to decide on a career, for instance, the White family wanted me to choose a profession that offered security. It is a natural desire for parents to want to guide their children in making career decisions. For me, the issue, however, was that I had no compass, no point of reference, such as an aunt or uncle or anyone within the extended family to inspire me or offer support in choosing a career, or direct me toward a talent that might have been present genetically within family confines. Both sides of my German family had seen generations of merchants, physicians and architects. My German mother, who herself had wanted to study medicine, lived vicariously through my intelligence and tried to steer me away from the arts, for which I had an affinity, to the sciences, which did not necessarily appeal to me. What I also created in my mind, was the idea that I had to be "White." As I saw it, White people lived successful lives through connections and without exerting much effort; the rest of the world had to work long and hard without an opportunity for a better life, regardless of effort. I was very conscious that my White parents' privilege rubbed off on me on many levels and at every stage, and I always embraced it. Except that there was one crucial drawback: while I knew how to be German, I did not know how to be Black and was uncomfortable among Blacks. I felt superior to Whites, but inferior to Blacks because I felt I could not fool them into thinking I was "one of them."

I've had various identities in my almost eight decades of life, and have enjoyed several professions that were each time predicated by external perceptions the world I lived in had placed on me. Now retired, widowed, with a son living in another state, I have time to look at my experience and try to come to some understanding of the emotionally layered, seemingly infinitely complex individual I've always been. In the end, the eternal question remains: Who am I, really?

When I approached my search for self without the interference of my family, I was about 21 years old. At first I think I felt vainly curious as I visited a palmist in Germany. Fascinated by the truths that were readable in my hands, I asked her to teach me her craft, which she did, because she saw my talent in Neptunian explorations. The shape of hands, the pattern of the lines, the marks in the inside of the palms reveal much about the personality, heritage, and potential future of a person. How we move our hands, how we hold them, belongs to the most basic and revelatory demeanors of interpretable body language.

A few days ago, displeased by the deformity of the middle finger of my right hand, where a year ago I had torn a tendon, I began to grapple about hands again. It struck me how the appearance of hands changes with age. It occurred to me that babies, in their tight little fists could well hold secrets in those closed hands. Secrets only they knew, such as the purpose for which they came to this life.

A baby's hand, when it holds onto someone's finger, has a very tight grip. Could it be sharing its information? Once the baby begins to see, it opens its little hands and begins to grasp for objects. It is becoming accustomed to the material world surrounding it, and so, slowly the mysteries from beyond begin to fade from memory. As much as I think babies and little children are cute, I have tended to be a somewhat leery of them. I keep my distance and observe them. Little children always look at me with significant intensity. I don't attribute it to my being dark, but to them looking at me as if wanting to share a wisdom I don't understand. After a while they smile broadly and reach out to me and wave. I wave back smiling; wondering what might have been imparted in our silent exchange. As they wave, I see the inside of their palms and recognize aspects of their personality.

Our hands change through the wear and tear of years. Older ones, most noticeably those impacted by crippling arthritis, intrigue me. Some older hands resemble the claws of birds. The owners symbolically holding on to the value of their possessions, or traditions, or the inability to shed the burden of false pride and shame. We all, to one extent or other, are burdened by our values and false pride and shame.

After death, when the spirit has left our body, our hands are open. There's nothing we can hold. By the law of the Universe we leave everyone and EVERYTHING behind that was dear and valuable to us, and to which our human experience made us cling with tenacity.

Sometimes I think of having willingly accepted an invitation to enter this life. Other times, I believe I deliberately chose this lifetime. Either way, it makes it easier to accept that the obstacles I had to deal with were lessons I needed to learn. What is the point of refusing to accept (as I did when I was much younger) things that were impossible to change; like my darker complexion and how others saw me and judged me.

Through the set of parents who gave us life, and the set that raised us and offered us their opportunities, as interracial adoptees we have genetic and social gifts. Despite our dark skin we know how to navigate the White world, and we can have Black friends through whom we learn about a history within the African Diaspora. Who else can claim that and has at their disposal that broader vision? We need to cherish our breadth as gifts to be used at every opportunity. Our feelings of abandonment and rejection, the many hurtful concealed messages we absorbed as children, are irretrievably in the past, but they all served a purpose; we learned how to act and react socially or genetically, or both. Each of us is as different as our experiences are unique. How we share our wisdom is also unique and should not be molded after anyone else's expectations.

Is it more difficult for interracial adoptees to trust our inner wisdom and the secrets we carried as babies in our fists? Are the layers of interference too thick to break through? Perhaps, perhaps not. But we must make an effort every day to take time to quiet our mind. Call it prayer or meditation, but through that practice we must try to reach that positive, uplifting, inner peace that is uniquely ours and offers us the unequaled strength only we, as individuals, understand.

I rise
I rise
I rise.

-Maya Angelou
And Still I Rise, Random House (New York, NY), 1978

CONTRIBUTOR BIOGRAPHIES

DR. NICHOLAS COOPER-LEWTER

REVEREND DR. NICHOLAS COOPER-LEWTER holds a Master of Social Work degree and a Ph.D. in Psychology. Throughout his four-decade plus career as a licensed psychotherapist, life coach, mental trainer, optimum performance professional, sports psychology researcher and expert, Dr. Nick is called the "Soul Whisperer," coaching hearts to empower minds and embrace their God-given potential. National and International Best Selling Author and Speaker, Dr. Nick is recognized for motivating others when sharing his adoption story and how he overcame childhood abuse. His work addressing multigenerational shame, trauma, grieving and the power of love has earned him international respect and recognition.

JOSHUA CROME

JOSHUA CROME is a transracial adoptee born in Chicago during the Baby Scoop Era. After four years of searching, he has been able to reunite with both sides of his natural family.

A #FlipTheScript re-tweeter and occasional poster, he is also a contributor to the *An-Ya Project's Flip The Script: Adult Adoptee Anthology*. Joshua is a magna cum laude graduate of Rider University, having majored in secondary education and history. He lives with his wife and children in New Jersey, and enjoys rooting for his beloved Chicago sports teams, golf, cooking on his charcoal pit, and cars.

APRIL DINWOODIE

As Chief Executive of the Donaldson Adoption Institute, April is committed to reframing perceptions about adoption and foster care adoption in order to improve laws, policies and practices through research, education and advocacy. She is the creator of a specialized mentoring program "Adoptment," where adults who were adopted and/or spent time in foster care mentor youth in care. She is also a co-founder of Fostering Change for Children. As a trans-racially adopted person, April shares her experiences to help adoptive parents, professionals and the public at large understand the complexities of race, class and culture in adoption.

AMANDINE GAY

AMANDINE GAY is a Montreal-based Afrofeminist filmmaker, activist, and journalist. In 2006, following her graduation from the Institute of Political Science in Lyon (France) with a masters in communication, Amandine joined the Conservatory of Dramatic Art in Paris 16. In 2014, she made her directorial debut with *Ouvrir La Voix* (Speak Up/Make Your Way), a feature-length documentary on European Black francophone women. She is also a contributor to the information website, Slate.fr. Most recently, Amandine authored the preface for the first French translation of bell hooks' seminal, *Ain't I A Woman*. She is currently completing her second master's degree in sociology, focusing on transracial adoption.

TARA LINH LEAMAN, JD

TARA LINH LEAMAN, JD is an African Vietnamese American transethnic adoptee, and is currently the Program Director of Westchester Building Futures, a multiyear federally-funded Westchester County Department of Social Services initiative that serves youth and young adults currently in foster care and/or alumni of care. She is also the Co-Founder of AmerAsians Building Bridges consulting, which provides training and resources that enrich the lives of members of the adoption and foster care constellations. She currently serves on the board of Holt International Children's Services and Family Equality Council's National Board of Advisers. Tara is a graduate of Cornell University and Georgetown Law.

NATASHA ORLANDO

NATASHA ORLANDO is a Midwestern TRA writer. She has a doctorate in American Studies, an MFA in creative writing, and teaches Africana Studies at a major Catholic university.

ROSEMARIE PEÑA

ROSEMARIE PEÑA is a dual-heritage, adoptee from Germany to the United States and identifies as a Black German-American. She is a PhD candidate in Childhood Studies at Rutgers University-Camden and holds two Bachelor degrees in Psychology and German, along with a Masters in Childhood Studies. Her research explores the historical and contemporary intersections of international adoption and migration. She is the founding president of the Black German Heritage and Research Association (BGHRA). Rosemarie is published in both English and German, and has delivered conference keynotes and presentations internationally on the post-World War II adoptions of Black German children.

JANET M. PRICE, PSYD

JANET M. PRICE, PSYD, is a bi-racial adoptee who was adopted transracially. She is also the adoptive mother of a bi-racial daughter, and two sons who joined the family through birth. Dr. Price has worked throughout her life to support children and families, both in the arena of adoption and additional areas. Janet received her first Master's degree in Special Education/ Early Childhood. Her doctoral studies focused on identity development for adoptees who become adoptive mothers. Janet has presented multiple times at the Adoption Conference of New England (ACONE) and taught pre-adoptive classes for an adoption agency in Maine. Currently Janet participates in a group therapy practice in Massachusetts as a clinical psychologist. Her clients include those touched by adoption, focusing on post-adoptive issues. Her therapeutic work also finds that issues such as inflexible-explosive behaviors, anxiety, depression, and Asperger's Syndrome find their way through her office door as well.

BARBARA ROBERTSON, LMSW

BARBARA ROBERTSON, LMSW is an adoptee who was born in Cleveland, Ohio and adopted in New York State where she currently resides. Due to the adoption records laws in Ohio, Barbara was unable to obtain a copy of her original birth certificate until new legislation took effect in 2015. She has since established contact with her biological parents, and has relationships with her mother, sister, and the maternal side of her family. She happily engages in her newest hobby, genealogy, and looks forward to continued family discoveries and connections. She is married and the mother of two sons.

ELIZABETH SEMONS

LIZ SEMONS is an adopted adult who was fostered for the first year and a half of her life. She is bi-racial. She now knows that she is black and Irish. Liz was adopted transracially. Her adoption experience came with many challenges, heartache, identity issues and eventually a huge miracle. Liz expresses herself best about her true emotions in the form of poetry and lyrics. She hopes to help make a difference in the adoption community through story and song.

SEAN SPARKS

SEAN SPARKS is a licensed marriage and family therapist and an adult adoptee who has provided adoption/foster care specific and trauma informed treatment through community based agencies for over 10 years. Sean has supervised adoption/foster care specific programs whose goal is increasing permanency for children in foster care and stabilizing adoptive placements that are at risk for disruption. Sean specializes in racial identity development and working with families who came together through transracial adoption. Sean provides consultation and training to caregivers and professionals about adoption/foster care informed clinical intervention and treatment.

DR. CATANA TULLY

Born in a remote village in Guatemala, actress, fashion model, painter, Professor Emerita of cultural studies, Catana Tully was adopted into a White German family, in 1940. Under layers of privilege, she later discovered that her greatest struggle was one of cultural and racial disinheritance. In her bestselling biography, *Split at the Root: A Memoir of Love and Lost Identity* she addresses issues related to cultural seduction and misplaced identity. This essay casts some light on a philosophy she created for herself, based on metaphysical studies that helped her find validation and purpose in her long and complex life.

HANNA WALLENSTEEN

HANNA WALLENSTEEN was born in Ethiopia and adopted to Sweden as an infant. She holds a Master of Science in Psychology from Stockholm University. Over the last 20 years Hanna has taken special interest in the various experiences of transracial adoptees. She gives lectures and seminars on the subject to teachers, social workers, therapists and people within the adoption community. Although Hanna regrets that she never learned Amharic, she loves the Swedish language and finds peace and joy in writing.

MILTON WASHINGTON

Born in South Korea, Milton was adopted and brought to the states in 1979 when and where he learned English and American culture. He's lived in Oklahoma, Virginia, Indiana, California, and Chicago and now lives in Harlem, New York where he raises his son Miles Pak Washington. A former college football player, he's now a partner in a boutique visual development and marketing agency called Knead Creative handing business development and sales. His ultimate passion is to empower others to be more empathetic through the power of storytelling.

MARIETTE WILLIAMS

MARIETTE WILLIAMS is a transracial adoptee born in Jeremie, Haiti. She was adopted at the age of three and grew up near Vancouver, B.C., Canada. In July of 2015, she reunited with her birth mother and several members of her birth family. She lives in South Florida with her husband and two children. In addition to being a Journalism and literature teacher, she writes essays, short stories, and poems that usually focus on adoption.

CHRISTOPHER THOMAS WILSON

CHRISTOPHER WILSON is the founder and president of CTW Productions. He honed his film and writing skills while attending Hawaii Pacific University. His entrepreneurial skills led him to become the CEO of 7one. As a filmmaker, his first feature length film *You Have His Eyes* continues to tour the United States and abroad. Wilson's personal journey has now become an award winning film dealing with the subject of adoption. His second feature length documentary will be released in 2017 and delves into the topic of mental health stigma. Wilson is part African American, Native American, French Canadian and German.

EDITORS

SUSAN HARRIS O'CONNOR, MSW

SUSAN HARRIS O'CONNOR, MSW is a pioneer and national leading voice on transracial adoption. Her groundbreaking autobiographical narratives are compiled in *The Harris Narratives: An Introspective Study of a Transracial Adoptee.* Since 1996, they have been performed over 100 times as keynote addresses, lectures and featured performances at places such as Harvard Medical Conference series, Smith College Summer Lecture series, Yale Law, Massachusetts General Hospital, NAACP, Starbucks Coffee, PACT Camp, Heritage Camp, Umoja and KAAN. Published by the Yale Journal of Law and Feminism and Adoption and Fostering, Susan received the 2014 Outstanding Practitioner in Adoption Award from St. John's University and the 2016 President's Award from American Adoption Congress.

DIANE RENÉ CHRISTIAN

DIANE RENÉ CHRISTIAN founded the *AN-YA Project* in 2012, after she published her debut novel, *An-Ya and Her Diary.*

As the founder of the *AN-YA Project*, Christian has edited/published—*An-Ya and her Diary: Reader & Parent Guide* as well as Co-edited/published *Perpetual Child: Adult Adoptee Anthology, Dismantling the Stereotype, Dear Wonderful You: Letters to Adopted & Fostered Youth* and *Flip the Script: Adult Adoptee Anthology.*

Black Anthology: Adult Adoptees Claim Their Space is the fifth book Christian has edited and published under the *AN-YA Project* umbrella.

MEI-MEI AKWAI ELLERMAN, PHD

MEI-MEI AKWAI ELLERMAN, PHD was born in NYC; adopted at 7 months. She lived in Europe until age 23. Harvard PhD in hand, she taught Italian literature and film for 30 years.

A scholar at the Brandeis Women's Studies Research Center, Mei-Mei is writing two memoirs: 1) on her decades-long search for her biological roots, 2) on her biracial adoptive mother's family history. Fierce activist, as Director Emerita of Polaris, she is deeply committed to fighting human trafficking and adoption-related rights.

As Co-founder of the *AN-YA Project*, recent publications include contributions co-editing *Dear Wonderful You, Letters to Adopted & Fostered Youth*, and contributing to the anthologies *Perpetual Child: Dismantling the Stereotype* and *Flip the Script: Adult Adoptee Anthology*. Mei-Mei also blogs on Chineseadoptee.com and is an avid photographer and Reiki master.

CPSIA information can be obtained
at www.ICGtesting.com
Printed in the USA
LVOW11s0938201116

513797LV00002B/372/P